Michael Price

Computer Basics

eighth edition

In easy steps is an imprint of In Easy Steps Limited
4 Chapel Court · 42 Holly Walk · Leamington Spa
Warwickshire · United Kingdom · CV32 4YS
www.ineasysteps.com

8th Edition

Notice of Liability

Every effort has been made to ensure that this book contains accurate
and current information. However, In Easy Steps Limited and the
author shall not be liable for any loss or damage suffered by readers
as a result of any information contained herein.

Trademarks

Microsoft® and Windows® are registered trademarks of Microsoft
Corporation. All other trademarks are acknowledged as belonging to
their respective companies.

In Easy Steps Limited supports The Forest Stewardship Council (FSC),
the leading international forest certification organisation. All our titles
that are printed on Greenpeace approved FSC certified paper carry the
FSC logo.

MIX
Paper from
responsible sources
FSC® C020837

Printed and bound in the United Kingdom

ISBN 978-1-84078-395-7

Contents

1 Choose a Computer

This chapter discusses the differences between computers – Mainframe and PC, laptop and desktop, Apple Mac and Windows – to help you choose your system.

What is a Computer?

Computers are essentially machines that accept sets of instructions (known as programs) and perform computations based on those instructions. The first computers were very large and demanded huge amounts of power. They were used for specialized calculations, such as trajectories (astronomical or military), code breaking or weather forecasting.

As they developed, computers were made smaller, less power-hungry and less expensive. This led to the introduction of personal computers, intended to support the requirements of individuals and small groups, not just business and government.

Although these machines may look old-fashioned, they included all the essential elements you'll find in every computer, in one form or another:

- Input   e.g.   keyboard and mouse
- Processing   manipulation and computation
- Output   display and print
- Storage   data and programs
- Operating System   to manage the data and programs
- Communications   links to other computers

These original computers illustrate the two main classes of personal computer – Apple Mac and IBM compatible. They also demonstrate the three main styles:

Desktop Computers

These are mains powered and have several individual components – display, keyboard and system unit (containing the processor, memory and storage elements). Literally desktop to begin with, the system unit is often effectively turned on its side to become a tower unit, which is placed beneath the desk.

Hot tip

The distinguishing factor between these is the operating system. IBM-compatibles run Microsoft Windows, while Apple Mac computers run the proprietary Mac OS.

Don't forget

This is a tower format IBM-compatible personal computer, the Dell Inspiron 580.

6

Laptop Computers

These are designed to be carried, and contain all of the components (including battery power) in one physical box. Some models emphasize lightness and ultra-portability, others offer the full function of a desktop computer in a space saving format.

All-in-One Computers

These machines are really a hybrid of the desktop and laptop machines, putting the components that are usually found in the system unit into the display housing. This provides a compact and stylish design, but these systems are not particularly portable, and they will need access to mains power.

Hot tip

These examples of laptop and all-in-one personal computers are from Apple, showing the Macbook and the iMac. There are also many IBM-compatible laptop and all-in-one computers.

Operating Systems

The operating system on the personal computer is software that manages the computer memory, storage, and devices, and provides an interface to access those resources. It processes data and user input, allocating and managing tasks and services for the user and the programs running on the system. It supports communication between computers and networks, and manages the files on the computer disk drives.

There are two predominant operating systems for personal computers, reflecting the two predominant types of personal computer:

Mac OS

This is a graphical operating system developed and marketed by Apple and pre-loaded on Apple Macintosh computers. The current version is Mac OS X, which is based on the Unix operating system used by larger scale computers.

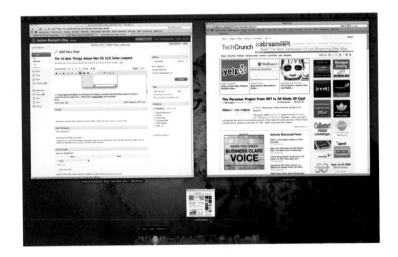

There are numerous applications and utilities supplied with Mac OS X. Other applications are available from Apple, Adobe, Microsoft and other suppliers.

Windows

This runs on all IBM-compatible computers, which account for over 90% of all personal computers, and it is by far the most commonly used operating system.

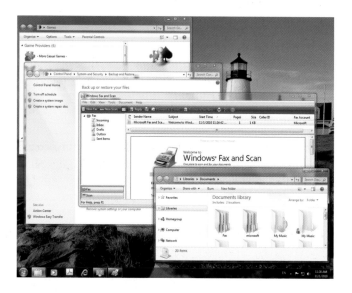

The current version is Windows 7, which is provided in a number of editions designed to suit particular types of user. For home and small office users, there are three editions:

- Windows 7 Starter
- Windows 7 Home Premium
- Windows 7 Ultimate

Two editions are provided for businesses and large organizations:

- Windows 7 Professional
- Windows 7 Enterprise

There is an edition that is designed for the users of personal computers in emerging technology markets:

- Windows 7 Home Basic

This edition is not available for PCs in the developed technology markets, such as the United States, European Union and Japan.

See page 26 for features of the main editions of Windows 7.

Beware

Starter Edition is for pre-installation only and has a number of restrictions, including no support for Aero and no Personalization.

Don't forget

Whichever edition of Windows 7 is installed on your computer, you will be able to upgrade it to a higher edition, with the Windows Anytime Upgrade feature.

PC Versus Mac

Don't forget

This is a subject that's sure to raise many strong opinions. Just saying "PC versus Mac" will create a huge debate about the scope of the term PC, with many insisting on the more explicit "IBM compatible PC" terminology.

Hot tip

The book uses Windows version 7 and Microsoft Office 2010 for the illustrations and the examples, but highlights differences with other environments when appropriate.

The best system for you depends on your particular requirements and circumstances, so there's no definitive answer. However, these are some of the factors you may wish to take into account when deciding between a Mac and an IBM compatible PC.

Design and Appearance

The PC is usually a fairly bland box of equipment, with some honorable exceptions, such as Sony's VAIO laptops.

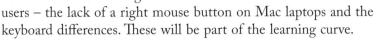

The Mac is generally considered to be the epitome of elegance and design. There are some issues that might disconcert PC users – the lack of a right mouse button on Mac laptops and the keyboard differences. These will be part of the learning curve.

Range of Options

PC system specifications are flexible and low end machines are likely to be cheaper, since there are competing brands, multiple suppliers and a variety of prices and quality levels. There's also a large choice of applications, since the majority of software is programmed for Windows systems.

With the Mac, there are limited choices of specification and you are essentially buying everything from the one company.

Specialized Systems

For some users, the single manufacturer approach becomes a strength, in niche areas such as the media industry for example. Publishing, film editing, photo editing and audio recording software products were developed for the Mac first (though these suites are now released on PC as well).

Robust Systems

The Mac features an operating system that is claimed to be simpler, more streamlined and more stable than Microsoft Windows. It is also more secure – perhaps because, as a minority product, it just doesn't get targeted as much by the malicious software threats that are endemic to Windows.

Gaming

If your main interest is gaming, a Windows PC is recommended. There's a much larger selection of games, hardware can be optimized for gaming performance, and new titles will always appear for the Windows machines first. There is no native DirectX support in Mac OS (although there are emulators).

Peer Support

If you don't already have experience with computers, you could well allow your choice to be influenced by your family, friends and potential computer teachers and follow their lead.

Office Functions

Both systems can be used for functions like Internet browsing, document manipulation, scheduling and multimedia playback, and they both support Office functions, such as word processing, spreadsheets and presentations. However, if you need to exchange documents with other users, check what they are using, to avoid compatibility problems. You'll find Windows is the most common system in use for Office applications.

Take Both Systems

If you really cannot make up your mind, and cost is not the issue, you can run either operating system on a Mac OS X machine, using the Boot Camp utility to dual boot the system, or using a virtual machine product. This will run a range of operating systems, including OS X, Vista and older operating systems, such as XP. This approach involves extra software license costs and either the reduced performance due to virtualization or the need to reboot between systems when you require a different application.

In Summary

Macs and PCs perform the same basic computer operations but there are differences in menu items offered, functions are found in different places and the keys and keystrokes used to perform particular operations are different. If you want to work with others, it will be most helpful if you all use the same operating environment, which is most likely to be the PC and Windows.

Don't forget

If you have serious computer enthusiasts among your friends, you may find that they are using one of the Linux operating systems, open software that is distributed without charge. Linux and open software applications are not directly compatible with Mac OS or Windows, but they can be run on PC or Mac systems, via dual boot or virtualization.

Don't forget

Windows also supports dual boot and virtual machine operations. However, Apple does not provide a stand-alone version of the Mac OS X operating system, so this cannot be installed on an IBM compatible PC.

Choosing a Laptop

If you need to travel with your PC, or need to minimize the space it takes up, you'll be looking for a laptop computer. The primary factor will be the weight – the more mobile you need to be, the lighter the laptop you'll want.

Dell, for example, group their laptops into three ranges by weight, and this in turn dictates the monitor sizes offered.

1 Ultra Light (< 5lbs)

Refine Your Search

⊟ Laptop Screen Size
- ☐ 10.1"
- ☐ 11" - 14"
- ☐ 15" - 16"
- ☐ 17" +

⊟ Laptop Weight
- ☑ < 5 lbs. (Ultra Light)
- ☐ 5 - 7 lbs. (Light)
- ☐ > 7 lbs. (Desktop Replacement)

The Inspiron Mini 1018 model is 10.5 by 7.8 ins by 1.0 to 1.3 ins (being slightly wedge shaped), starts off at 2.2 lbs, and features a 160GB disk drive. The screen size is 10.1 ins.

2 Light (5 - 7lbs)

Refine Your Search

⊟ Laptop Screen Size
- ☐ 10.1"
- ☐ 11" - 14"
- ☐ 15" - 16"
- ☐ 17" +

⊟ Laptop Weight
- ☐ < 5 lbs. (Ultra Light)
- ☑ 5 - 7 lbs. (Light)
- ☐ > 7 lbs. (Desktop Replacement)

With a larger 17.3 ins screen, the Inspiron 17R is 16.5 by 10.9 ins by 1.4 ins and weighs 6.72 lbs or more.

The XPS 14 (with a 14 ins screen and 5.72 lbs) and the Inspiron 15 (15.6 ins screen and 5.8 lbs) provide alternative choices for mid range laptops.

There are various options, for each model, such as case colors, more powerful processors, extra system memory and enhanced graphics.

Don't forget

You can also select your choices for screen size, processor, price band, memory size, speed, storage, video type, or optical drive options, to further control the range of laptops presented.

Refine Your Search

⊞ Laptop Screen Size

⊞ Processor

⊞ Price

⊞ Memory

⊞ How fast does it need to be?

⊞ How much storage do you need?

⊞ Video Card Type

⊞ Laptop Weight

⊞ Optical Drive

3 Desktop Replacement (> 7lbs)

Refine Your Search

☐ Laptop Screen Size
- ☐ 10.1"
- ☐ 11" - 14"
- ☐ 15" - 16"
- ☐ 17" +

☐ Laptop Weight
- ☐ < 5 lbs. (Ultra Light)
- ☐ 5 - 7 lbs. (Light)
- ☑ > 7 lbs. (Desktop Replacement)

Don't forget

The larger laptops forgo some aspects of portability in favor of screen size and configuration options, such as Blu-Ray disc drives and dedicated graphics memory.

For desktop replacements, the XPS 17 (17.3 ins screen and from 7.94 lbs) is available in a variety of configurations, including 1 TB (1000 GB) hard drive, 8 GB memory and a Blu-ray drive.

The Alienware M15x, which has a 15.6 ins screen and a starting weight of 9 lbs, includes advanced graphics and a high power quad core processor. This allows it to act as a very robust replacement for a desktop gaming computer.

Other Factors

Battery life may range from 2 or 3 hours for the higher powered machines to 7 or more for the lower powered. Supplementary batteries may be available to increase the usable time between recharges.

Most machines will offer a rewritable DVD drive, or perhaps a combination DVD/CD-RW drive, but you are unlikely to find a floppy drive. However, you can usually purchase an add-on USB drive if you still need access to floppy disks.

The Windows 7 Starter edition may be included with mini or netbook computers, while laptop computers usually have the fuller function Windows 7 Home Premium edition.

Hot tip

Some models of laptop include a second drive bay, which can be used for an additional battery.

Desktop Computers

Don't forget

You'll usually be able to choose between budget and high-end ranges, in Dell's case, Inspiron and XPS for home and home office users.

Hot tip

For all but the most basic requirements, choose 4 GB memory and a dedicated graphics card with 256MB or more memory installed.

If you don't need a portable computer, you'll find that the desktop options give you much more choice of monitors, processors, graphics, memory, hard drive and optical drives. To illustrate the options available:

Refine Your Search

⊟ Processor
- ☑ Intel Celeron
- ☐ Intel Core 2 Duo
- ☐ Intel Core i3
- ☐ Intel Core i5
- ☐ Intel Core i7
- ☐ AMD

⊟ Desktop Monitor Size
- ☐ No Monitor
- ☐ 19" - 20" (Medium)
- ☐ Over 20" (Large)

⊟ Memory
- ☐ More than 4GB
- ☐ 4GB
- ☐ 3GB
- ☑ 2GB

⊞ How much storage do you need?

⊟ Video Card Type
- ☐ Integrated Graphics
- ☐ Dedicated Video Card

⊞ Price

⊟ Optical Drive
- ☐ CD/DVD+RW
- ☐ Blu-Ray Disc

⊟ Form Factor
- ☐ All-in-one
- ☑ Mini Tower
- ☐ Slim Tower
- ☐ Performance and Gaming

⊞ How fast does it need to be?

1 Select basic specifications, for a PC such as the Inspiron 560, for email, Internet surfing and documents

2 Choose higher specifications, for a PC like the Aurira ALX, for multitasking, playing music, watching videos, running graphics programs or playing games

You can adjust the configuration for the selected model by choosing alternative components, such as monitor, graphics card or hard disk. You can also include add-on items like a TV tuner, networking device, web camera, printer and scanner.

All-in-One

To get the space-saving benefits of laptops and the flexible configuration options of the desktop, choose an all-in-one design, such as the Dell XPS One.

Hot tip

This incorporates a 23 ins 1080P HD wide screen monitor with integrated 2 MB webcam, microphone and stereo speakers.

There's just a monitor on a stand, a wireless keyboard and mouse and a remote control. Everything else is included in the monitor, e.g. hard disk, CD/DVD re-writer, six USB ports, a 7 in 1 media card reader, audio input/output, network ports and TV input.

Don't forget

There is built-in wireless networking, with RF, IR, WiFi and Bluetooth, plus Gigabyte Ethernet.

There's a standard model and a performance model, and each of these can be confgured with the optional multitouch display. This allows you to toggle between windows with the swipe of a finger. You can also zoom in and out of photos and websites, and take advantage of touch-optimized applications. TouchCam lets you edit and upload photos and video directly to Facebook or YouTube. StickyNotes lets you write a note or type a message. Cyberlink YouPaint and other touch games are provided to entertain younger users.

Hot tip

Dell Stage, available on touch screen systems only, helps you organize your music, photos and videos, share photos on Facebook, and even listen to your favorite radio station, all at your fingertips.

Help with Selecting

Hot tip

We've used Dell to show how you can zero in on the computer that best fits your requirements, but all the suppliers are equally keen to help you find your way through the range of alternatives.

Don't forget

Dell will also suggest some alternative, higher powered solutions that may also suit.

MORE POWER
XPS 15
$949.99

BEST PERFORMANCE
XPS 17
$1,049.99

For more specific help in choosing your computer:

1 Visit www.dell.com, and click For Home

2 Scroll down to the Need Help Shopping section and click Get Recommendations

3 You can define the system in terms of what is important to you, and specify the computer type and price range

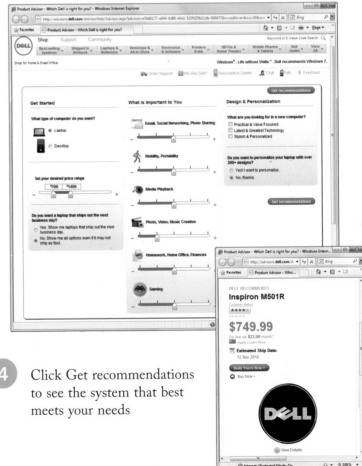

4 Click Get recommendations to see the system that best meets your needs

2 Explore Your Computer

We explore a typical computer to identify the hardware components involved, the operating system and its features and the additional software , including office applications and other useful programs, tools and utilities supplied with Windows 7.

The Example Computer

For the purposes of illustration, we will use a Dell Inspiron 560 computer. This is a desktop PC aimed at the home and small office user in particular.

This computer includes the following main components:

The Display

The monitor attached to the computer is the Dell ST2210 21.5 ins wide-screen display with a full HD resolution of 1920 x 1080 pixels.

The Keyboard

By default, the system will use a standard USB cable-connected keyboard with 104 keys (105 keys on European versions).

The Mouse

The mouse used is the typical 2-button optical scroll wheel mouse, which, like the keyboard, uses USB cable and port for connection.

The System Unit

This is a mini tower model that is designed for vertical use. The system unit includes a 2.5 GHz Intel Core 2 Quad processor with 6 GB memory.

There's a 1 TB (1024 GB) hard disk drive and a 10/100/1000 Ethernet adapter.

Don't forget

Since there is more than 256MB memory assigned to the graphics adapter, this system will support the Windows Aero functions.

The DVD/CD re-writer drive is accessed from the front panel, where there's also space for a second optical drive.

Below the two drive bays, in the location that might previously have been assigned to the floppy, drive there are microphone and headphone connectors and a pair of USB ports. There may also be an optional 19 in 1 media card reader.

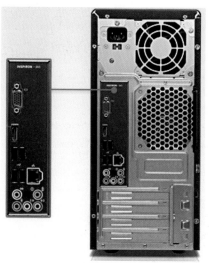

The rear of the unit includes the power socket, voltage selector and connections panel. This has the VGA and HDMI connectors for the integrated graphics adapter, the audio sockets, the network port and four additional USB ports.

Hot tip

There are slots for up to four hardware adapter cards, one of which is used for the ATI Radeon graphics adapter.

The integrated graphics adapter can be over-ridden by a separate adapter, the ATI Radeon 5450 in this case, which includes 1 GB graphics memory and connectors for VGA, DVI and HDMI.

Computer Configuration

When you start up the computer with its Windows 7 operating system, it normally displays one of the Windows 7 themes as the background, plus any desktop icons or gadgets that may be active.

Don't forget

This shows Windows 7 Home Premuium edition with the Aero display functions in operation. Your computer may be supplied with another edition, such as Professional or Ultimate, which also support Aero.

Hot tip

For subsequent screen images, the background will be changed to plain white to improve clarity.

 1 For details of your system, select Start, Computer

This gives an overview of the storage devices on your computer - the hard disk (drive C:) and the DVD re-writer (drive D:). Drive letters E:, F:, G: and H: are assigned to the media card reader device. It also shows your document libraries.

Hot tip

There are four entries for Portable Devices, reflecting the four slots in the media card reader.

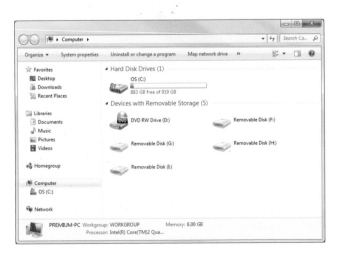

2 Select the System Properties button from the Computer window

The System window shows details like the processor type, memory and system level. It also shows the system performance rating, a value of 5.1 in this case.

3 Click Windows Experience Index to display details of the rating

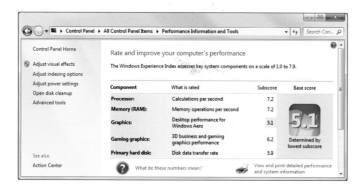

The base system rating is set as the lowest of the individual scores for the processor, the main memory, the graphics, 3D business and gaming graphics and the primary hard disk. These help to identify which components need to be enhanced to achieve an increase in overall performance.

Device Manager

1 Select the Device Manager link from the menu at the left of the System details

2 Click the ▷ next to a heading to expand the list (or double-click the heading itself)

3 Click the ◢ next to a heading (or double-click the heading) to collapse the list of entries

Don't forget

Under Processor, you will see two entries for dual processors, and four entries for quad processors.

4 Select an entry, and options are added to the toolbar to update driver software, and uninstall or disable the device

Beware

If you are prompted for an administrator password or to confirm the action, you must type the password or provide confirmation before proceeding.

Windows Anytime Upgrade

As well as showing the current edition, the System window also provides a link to get a new edition of Windows (unless you are already at the Ultimate level).

Beware

Check that your system has the appropriate capabilities for the new edition, especially if your existing system is the Windows 7 Starter.

1 Select the link and go on-line to purchase an edition

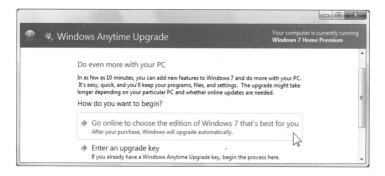

2 You are offered the upgrades appropriate for your edition

Don't forget

You'll be shown the editions and upgrade prices for your existing system. The features for the editions are also shown (see page 26).

25

Operating System Features

There are some features of Windows 7 that are included only in the more advanced editions, for example.

Features / Editions	ST	HP	Pro	Ult
Make things you do every day easier with improved desktop navigation	X	X	X	X
Start programs faster and easier, and quickly find documents you use often	X	X	X	X
Make your web browsing faster, easier and safer with Internet Explorer 8	X	X	X	X
Basic Games (FreeCell, Hearts, Spider etc)	X	X	X	X
Premium Games (Internet Backgammon, Checkers, Spades and Mahjong Titans)		X	X	X
64-bit processor support		X	X	X
Fast User Switching		X	X	X
Watch your favorite DVD movies		X	X	X
Personalize your desktop with custom backgrounds, colors, and sounds		X	X	X
Access photos, movies, and videos from a Windows 7 PC anywhere in the world		X	X	X
Watch, pause, rewind, and record selected TV programs on your PC		X	X	X
Easily create a home network and connect your PCs to a printer with Homegroup			X	X
Run many Windows XP productivity programs in Windows XP Mode			X	X
Connect to company networks easily and more securely with Domain Join			X	X
Back up your computer to a home or business network			X	X
Protect data on your PC and portable devices from loss or theft with BitLocker				X
Work in the language of your choice and switch between any of 35 languages				X
Windows Anytime Upgrade	X	X	X	

Make sure that the edition of Windows 7 you choose supports the features you will want to use.

Programs Included

Windows 7 manages your monitor, mouse and keyboard and all the devices incorporated into your computer. You'll find many of these functions in the Control Panel.

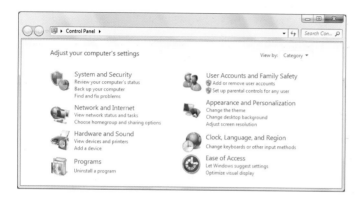

Windows 7 also includes a whole series of programs to help you carry out the tasks that justified your purchase. The main Windows programs and Accessories are displayed in the Start menu (see page 41) and include the following:

Don't forget

There are additional programs, tools, utilities, games and functions to be found in other Start menu subfolders, eg:

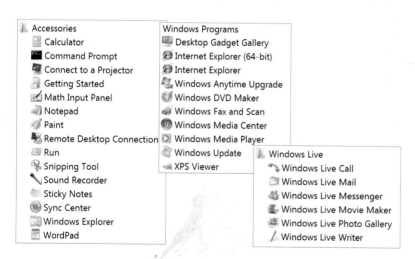

27

Some applications originally provided with Windows must now be downloaded (at no charge) from the Microsoft Windows Live website at http://explore.live.com/windows-live-essentials.

The built-in or downloaded programs provide valuable functions for most purposes, but, for the more demanding requirements, you may need a full office package (see page 29).

Microsoft Office Starter

Your system may be supplied with Microsoft Office 2010 Starter. To activate this:

1 Select Start, then Microsoft Office 2010

2 Choose the option to use Office Starter

The Starter edition has two programs. Word Starter and Excel Starter, plus some office tools.

3 Select Start, and click Microsoft Office Starter

Microsoft Office Starter (English)
Microsoft Excel Starter 2010
Microsoft Word Starter 2010
Microsoft Office 2010 Tools

4 Choose the Microsoft Word Starter 2010 application

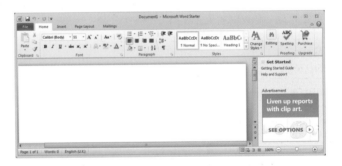

5 Similarly, you can start the Excel Starter 2010 application

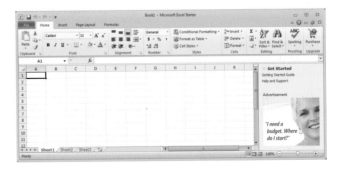

Microsoft Office

For a more robust set of office applications, you'd use Microsoft Office, the latest version being Microsoft Office 2010. There are six main editions, each with its own selection of applications. The Starter and Web editions are also shown for comparison:

Editions / Applications	Starter	Home & Student	Home & Business	Standard	Professional & Academic	Professional Plus	Web
Word	Y	Y	Y	Y	Y	Y	Y
Excel	Y	Y	Y	Y	Y	Y	Y
PowerPoint	-	Y	Y	Y	Y	Y	Y
OneNote	-	Y	Y	Y	-	Y	Y
Outlook	-	-	Y	Y	Y	Y	-
Publisher	-	-	-	Y	Y	Y	-
Access	-	-	-	-	Y	Y	-
InfoPath	-	-	-	-	-	Y	-
SharePoint Workspace	-	-	-	-	-	Y	-
Communicator	-	-	-	-	-	Y	-
MapPoint 2010	-	-	-	-	-	-	-
Project	-	-	-	-	-	-	-
Visio	-	-	-	-	-	-	-

1 Click Start, All Programs and select Microsoft Office to see the applications available

2 Click Microsoft Office Tools to list additional programs and utilities provided with Office

Microsoft Office
- Microsoft Access 2010
- Microsoft Excel 2010
- Microsoft InfoPath Designer 2010
- Microsoft InfoPath Filler 2010
- Microsoft OneNote 2010
- Microsoft Outlook 2010
- Microsoft PowerPoint 2010
- Microsoft Publisher 2010
- Microsoft SharePoint Workspace 2010
- Microsoft Word 2010
- Microsoft Office 2010 Tools

Don't forget

Professional Plus and Standard editions have Outlook plus Business Contact Manager (BCM). The other editions have Outlook alone.

Hot tip

Some of the Microsoft Office applications are only available as individual products, not as part of a suite.

Beware

You'll only see this set of applications if you have the Professional Plus edition of Office 2010 installed on your system.

Adobe Reader

There's a huge variety of software available for Windows-based computers, tailored to meet particular needs and requirements. Many such products can be downloaded from the Internet, often at no charge. Here is one that will prove particularly useful:

1 Go to **www.adobe.com**, locate the Download section and click Adobe Reader

2 Clear the box for the Google Toolbar, since this is not a requirement for Adobe Reader

3 Scroll down, click the Download Now button, then follow the prompts to download, install and configure the Reader

AVG Antivirus

If your computer does not have anti-virus software installed, you could try the free edition of the AVG Antivirus program.

1 At website free.grisoft.com click Download Now for the AVG Antivirus free edition 2011

2 Click the Download button for Anti-Virus Free Edition

3 Follow the prompts to download and install the AVG antivirus program

4 Once installed, AVG will automatically apply the latest updates and will refresh the data files on a daily basis

Don't forget

The AVG Antivirus Free Edition provides basic antivirus and anti-spyware protection for Windows, for home and non-commercial use.

Hot tip

At each stage, you'll be offered one of the higher function chargeable editions. However, the free edition should be sufficient in most cases.

IrfanView

The third recommended application is the IrfanView graphic viewer. This is a small, compact and very fast freeware application for non-commercial use, which runs under most versions of Windows, including Windows 7.

 Go to website **www.irfanview.com** and click the link to download the current version of IrfanView

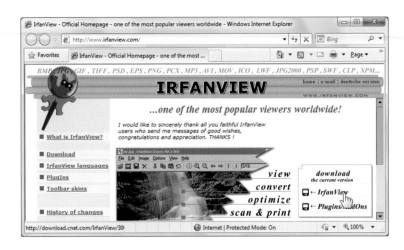

2 This application is available from the CNET website **download.com**. Click the Download Now link

 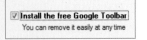
3 Follow the prompts to complete the installation and launch the IrfanView program

3 Windows Basics

Here we look more closely at Windows 7 and the ways in which you can control its appearance and manage the systems and applications windows. The differences between Windows 7 Basic and Windows 7 Aero are explained. Finally, we look at the types of user accounts Windows provides and how you add new users.

Windows Display

What you see on your computer depends on which version of Windows you have installed, the updates that have been applied, and any customization that has been carried out. So don't be surprised if things are not exactly the same as illustrated here.

However, the differences are more in the appearance than in how Windows behaves. All versions of Windows use the same basic skills and approaches, though things may vary in their effects and details may be rearranged.

There are two main sections – the desktop and the taskbar.

The Desktop

Icons and Shortcuts   Application Windows   Desktop Area   Windows Sidebar

Start Button   Shortcuts   Active Tasks   Notification Area

There may be additional system icons in the Notification area. To see these:

1. Click the Show hidden icons button on the left of the Notification area

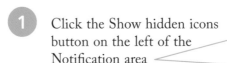

2. A panel with the extra icons will be displayed

Desktop Themes

There's usually a picture or image shown as the background to the desktop. You can change this and adjust the windows color, sound and screen saver all at the same time, by selecting a desktop theme.

1. Right-click an empty area on the desktop and select Personalize

2. Select an Aero theme like Landscapes to replace the default Windows 7 theme

3. The selected theme is applied immediately

Alternatively, you can select images from your Pictures folder to act as the desktop background.

Desktop Background
Harmony

1. Select Personalize and click Desktop Background to change the existing image

2. Browse to the picture folder and select one or more images, which are then assigned as the background

3. For the purposes of the book, a plain white image is selected

Don't forget

When you have multiple images as background, they will be swapped periodically (or you can select Next desktop background, the entry that gets added to the right-click menu).

Screen Resolution

The screen resolution governs the clarity and the size of the screen contents. At higher resolutions (e.g. 1920 x 1200) items are smaller and sharper, and more items can be displayed. At low resolutions (e.g. 800 x 600) items appear larger, fewer items can be displayed and the overall image may appear less precise.

To adjust the screen resolution:

Hot tip

The values that are offered depend on the configuration. The laptop screen shown offers values including:

1920 x 1200	8x5
1680 x 1050	8x5
1440 x 900	8x5
1280 x 800	8x5
1280 x 720	16x9
800 x 600	4x3

Display ratios other than the physical ratio (8x5 in this case) may distort the image, e.g. make circles appear oval.

1 Select Screen Resolution from the desktop right-click menu, or select Start, Control Panel and click Adjust screen resolution from Appearance and Personalization

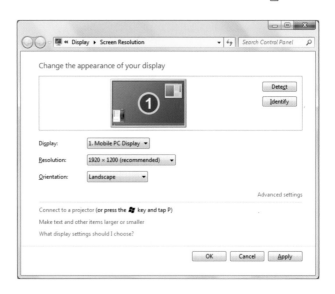

2 Click the Resolution box, select a resolution, then click Apply, OK

3 Click Keep changes to confirm

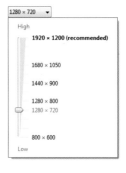

Don't forget

You can also change the orientation from Landscape to Portrait, useful if you have a monitor that can be rotated.

Dual Monitors

If your graphics adapter supports dual monitors, you can attach a
second monitor, which can be sized and orientated independently.

1 Click Detect,
then select the
1st monitor

2 Select the 2nd
monitor

3 Click the Multiple displays box to specify how the
displays are to be used.

You can duplicate the displays, extend the desktop across them
both, or show the desktop only on one or the other.

1 Click Identify to check the physical alignment

Note that the taskbar appears on the main display when you
extend the desktop across the two monitors.

Beware

If your monitor supports
multiple connections, do
not attempt to use both
connections on the same
computer.

Hot tip

You can drag an
application window
across both screens.

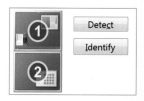

Don't forget

Drag one of the screens
to reposition them, in
the opposite sequence
or vertically instead of
horizontally.

Mouse Settings

You can change the way that the mouse pointer appears and how it behaves when clicking and selecting.

1 Select Personalize from the desktop right-click menu, then select the task to Change mouse pointers

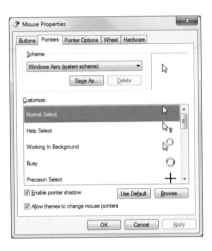

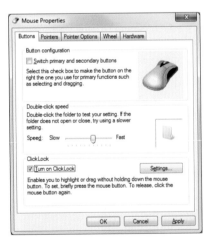

2 From the Pointers tab, choose a mouse pointer scheme, enable or disable pointer shadows and customize specific pointers

3 Click the Buttons tab and select the box to exchange the primary and secondary (left and right) buttons

4 Click on the folder to check double-click speed, and drag the slider to adjust the speed

5 Click the box to turn on the ClickLock option, and click the Settings button adjust the sensitivity

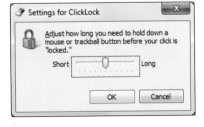

6 Click the Pointer Options tab to adjust the pointer speed and to enhance the pointer precision

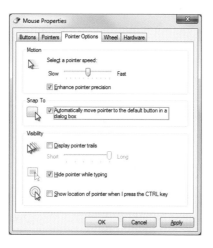

7 Click the SnapTo box to automatically move the mouse pointer to the default button when you open a dialog box

8 You can help keep track of the position of the mouse pointer by enabling pointer trails, or by choosing to show the pointer location when you press the Ctrl key

9 Click the Wheel tab to review or change actions using the mouse wheel (if there's one fitted on your mouse)

Starting Windows

When you turn on your computer, the system initializes and then displays the Logon screen, with the user names that are defined.

1 Click on the user name required for this session

2 Type the associated password and press the Enter key (or click the arrow) to display the Windows desktop

3 Click the Start button to display the Start Menu

Start Menu

Predefined Programs   Recently Used Programs   Picture for Selected item (or user account)

Current User Name

User Folders

Computer details

Control Panel

Help function

Search Box   Taskbar   Shutdown Functions

The Shutdown functions provide options to turn off your computer, temporarily or fully, or to switch user names, etc.

1 Click Start and then click the Shutdown button to turn off your computer

2 Click the arrow next to Shutdown to display the alternative options

3 Choose to Switch user, Log off the current user name, Lock your computer in a secure state, shutdown and Restart, Sleep or Hibernate

| Switch user |
| Log off |
| Lock |
| Restart |
| Sleep |
| Hibernate |

Shut down ▷

41

Hot tip

You can also display the Start Menu by pressing one of the Windows Logo keys, found next to the Ctrl keys on the keyboard.

Don't forget

When you select Sleep or Hibernate, Windows places the computer into an energy-saving mode, which automatically saves open documents and turns off all non-essential functions. When you restart, it quickly returns to the point where you were.

Open a Window

Hot tip

There are a number of ways to open a window for a program, a folder or a file. The first three methods shown make use of the Start Menu, but there are also other techniques.

1. Select one of the fixed links, one of the predefined or recently used programs or a folder, from the lists on the top level of the Start Menu (as shown on page 41)

2. Click All Programs, then scroll through the menus, clicking submenus to open them if necessary. Locate and select the required entry

3. Type part of the name into the Search box and select the desired program, folder or file from the list of matches that gets displayed

4. Select a shortcut entry from the Quick Launch bar

Don't forget

Click the Show Desktop button on the Taskbar to minimize all windows and reveal the desktop, so you can select a program or file icon.

5. Double-click an icon in a folder or on the desktop to open a window with the associated program

6. Right-click a file in a folder or on the desktop, select Open With and choose a suitable application from the list offered. For example, a Word file may offer options like these

Window Structures

When you open a folder, it opens a window that displays the contents of that folder as file or folder icons. Programs open as windows that are specific to the particular application. There will be differences but the windows share many features in common.

Folder Window

Forward and Back   Folder Path   Search Box   Minimize Maximize/Restore

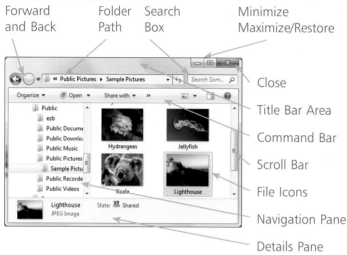

Close

Title Bar Area

Command Bar

Scroll Bar

File Icons

Navigation Pane

Details Pane

Hot tip

These file icons are in the form of Thumbnail icons (miniature images). Click the Views button to switch between List, Details and Tile icons.

43

Program/File Window

Right-click a picture file icon and open it with a suitable program, Windows Paint in this case. You will find that this application window uses the Title bar at the top. Below, this is the tab bar. There are also ribbon toolbars and a color palette. There are two scroll bars as the picture is larger than the available image area.

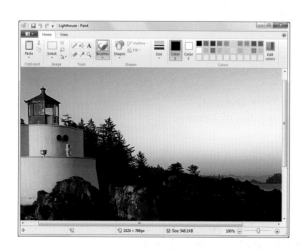

Don't forget

Some applications, Notepad for example, preserve the windows style from previous versions of Windows, e.g. the File, Edit menu bar, rather than the tab and ribbon style shown.

Move and Resize Windows

To reposition a folder or application window on the screen:

1 Move the mouse pointer over the title bar, then click and drag the window to the required location

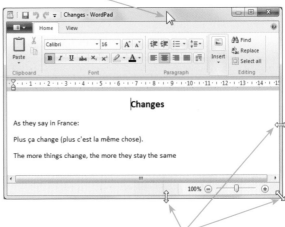

44

2 Click and drag an edge to resize the window horizontally or vertically, or click a corner to resize in two directions

To avoid moving the contents of the window while dragging:

1 Open the System Properties and select Windows Experience Index (see page 23), then click Adjust visual effects

2 Clear the box Show windows contents while dragging

3 An outline is displayed and moved until the move or resize is completed

Select a Window (Basic)

When you have numerous windows open on your desktop, you need functions to help you switch to the one you want next. The methods depend on the Windows interface. If you have selected Windows 7 Basic as your desktop theme (see page 35), or if you have the Starter edition installed, you have these options:

(see page 35)

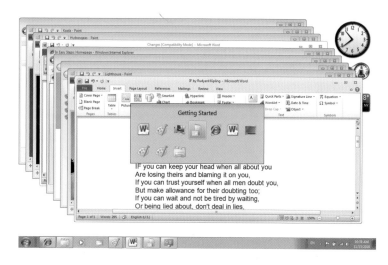

1. Press Alt+tab to display the window icons, then press tab repeatedly to choose the required window

2. Pause the mouse pointer over an entry on the taskbar and the full program and document names are shown

3. If there are multiple tasks grouped together, click the group and the individual items are displayed

Select a Window (Aero)

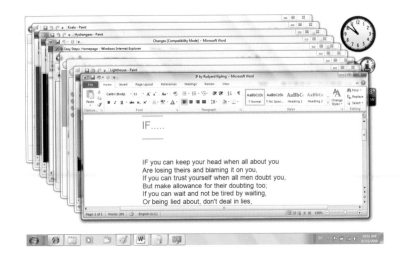

1 Press Alt+tab and press Tab repeatedly to select a window

2 Pause the mouse pointer over an entry on the taskbar and a thumbnail of the window will be displayed

3 If there are multiple tasks for the program, a thumbnail for each instance will be displayed

4 Select a thumbnail to switch to the associated window

5 Press the Windows Logo Key + Tab and all windows are displayed in a stack format known as Flip 3D

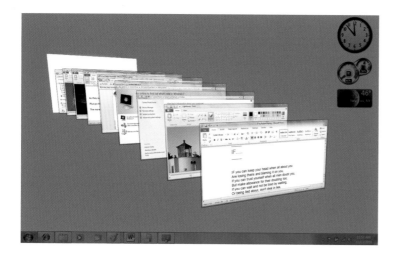

6 Hold down Windows Logo and press Tab repeatably to flip through the set of windows, one by one

7 When the required window is at the front, release the Windows Logo key, that window will then become current

Close a Window

There are a number of different ways to close windows when you have finished with them. To close a specific window, choose one of these methods:

1 Select the window to make it the active window, then click the Close button on the right of the title bar

2 To close the window from the taskbar, display the task thumbnail and click the Close button

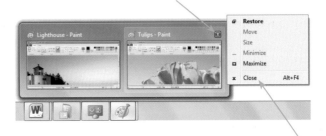

3 Right-click the thumbnail and select the Close option

4 Right-click the task icon to show the Jump List and select Close window or (where there are multiple tasks) Close all windows

Saving Changes

If any window you close contains modified information, you'll be prompted to save the associated document or file before going on to close the window itself.

New User Account

You'll need an extra user account if your main user account has been set up with full administrator privileges. You may also need accounts for other users of the computer, to help keep your emails and documents separate. To add an account:

1 Select Start, Control Panel and select Add or remove user accounts, from User Accounts and Family Safety

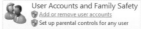

2 Select the entry to Create a new account

3 Provide the account name and choose the account type. This should normally be Standard, although you do need an Administrator account for system actions

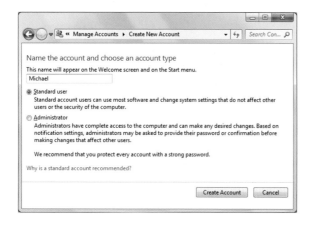

Hot tip

You could also double-click Add New Users in Getting Started to open the user accounts area.

49

Don't forget

You can enable the more restrictive Guest account for casual users of your computer.

Hot tip

Make sure you know the password for your Administrator level account, since this is often all that's needed to confirm authority for system tasks.

Windows Basics

...cont'd

Don't forget

If you have an administrator account, you can change the settings, including passwords, for any user on the computer.

4 To make changes to the settings, click on the new entry

5 You can change the account name, picture or type, you can also Create a password

Don't forget

If you sign on using a standard account, you can only modify the password and the picture associated with that account. Any other actions will require an administrator account ID and password.

6 Type a password and enter it again to confirm. The password should be 8 or more characters, a mix of upper and lower case letters, symbols and numbers. Don't use actual names or complete words

4 Word Processing

Use your word processor to create letters, memos and reports. Add interest and emphasis to your documents by using different fonts and adding illustrations. Learn the basic skills and how to use the standard tools provided in the word processor, which can be transferred to other applications. For example, add pictures and clip art, or use templates for documents.

Word Processors

Word processing is a basic computer function. It has been a feature since PCs first came into being, but has grown dramatically in functionality and ease of use. It can be used to create anything from a simple memo through to a complex manuscript, complete with illustrations, indexes and footnotes.

Hot tip

Notepad and WordPad can be found by clicking Start, All Programs, Accessories.

Notepad

Supplied with all versions of Windows, this is a basic text processor. It enables you to create and save generic text documents that have no formatting so can be read by virtually any word processor. Notepad documents are used by many software manufacturers to create soft copy manuals and instruction booklets and have the file suffix .txt.

notepad

WordPad

WordPad is a limited function word processor, also included with all editions of Windows. If all you wished to do was create simple documents, with some degree of layout and font enhancements, it would be sufficient.

wordpad

Word Starter

This is part of Office Starter, an ad-supported product that includes Word Starter and Excel Starter. These are reduced-function versions for viewing, editing, and creating documents. Office Starter is only available preloaded on Windows PCs. Word Starter offers many text formatting capabilities but lacks features found in Word itself, such as SmartArt, tracked changes, comments, macros and add-ons.

Microsoft Word Starter 2010

Don't forget

An online version of Word can be accessed, at no charge, by visiting office.live.com and registering for SkyDrive and the Microsoft Office Web Applications.

Microsoft®
Office
2010
WEB APPLICATIONS

W   X   P   N
Word Excel PowerPoint OneNote

Word

Word is a full function word processor, so you can create professional documents and add indexes, captions and tables of figures. You can specify languages and dictionaries, insert standard text and create bibliographies. There are many ease of use functions, and you can extend its capabilities by using macros and add-ons. Since it is the most widely used word processing product, it is easy to share your Word documents with other users.

Microsoft Word 2010

Create a Document

Although we are using Word to illustrate the word processing window, all the word processing products mentioned on the previous page will appear very similar and behave in much the same way as when simply entering text.

1 When you open the word processor, you will see the cursor flashing at the start of the document, indicating the point where the typing will begin

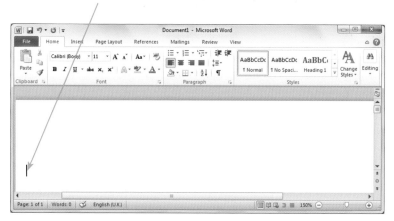

2 The text automatically wraps to the next line as you type

3 Press the Enter or Return key to start a new paragraph

4 Press the Caps Lock key to get all capitals, or the Shift key to get individual capitals (works with alphabetic keys only)

5 Press the Shift key to get the character shown on the top of non-alphabetic keys (even when the Caps Lock key is on)

Hot tip

When you open Word, the Home tab is selected, providing access to the most used functions, such as font formats, text alignments and editing facilities.

Don't forget

The keyboard layout shown is for US keyboards. International keyboards have different keys and arrangements.

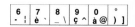

53

Don't forget

The numeric keypad on the right of the keyboard has two functions – numbers and navigation. To get numbers, the Num Lock key indicator must be lit.

Layout Your Page

Your word processor has certain settings already defined. These are known as the default settings and include items like font styles and sizes and the page layout options, such as margins, line spacing and page orientation.

To change the page layout:

1 Select the Page Layout tab and click the Margins option. Several standard settings are offered, including narrow, wide and mirrored margins

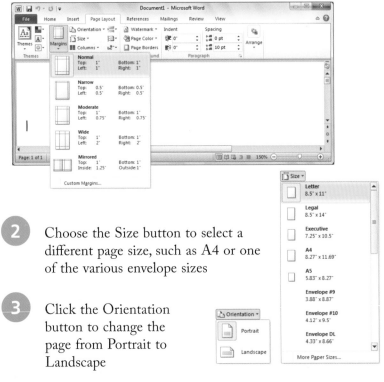

2 Choose the Size button to select a different page size, such as A4 or one of the various envelope sizes

3 Click the Orientation button to change the page from Portrait to Landscape

4 Select the View tab and tick the Ruler box to display the horizontal and vertical rulers around the typing area

Navigate the Document

In normal typing mode, Word can only display a screenful of typing at a time. You can use the following methods to move around the document:

1. Press the Home key to move the cursor to the left margin and the End key to move to the end of the line

2. Press the Ctrl+Home keys together (press the Ctrl key first) to move swiftly to the beginning of the document and Ctrl+End to move to the end of the document

3. Press the Page Down key to move down a screenful of text and the Page Up key to do the reverse

4. Select the View tab to access functions, such as Zoom in on the document or view one or two whole pages at once

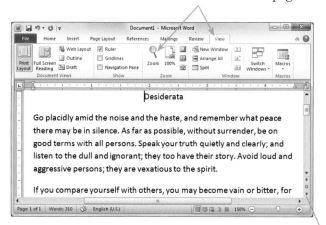

5. Use the Page Navigation icons to move through the document one page at a time

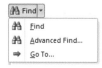

6. On the Home tab, click Find and Go To, to specify a particular page number

Don't forget

If you have a mouse with a scrolling wheel, you can use that to scroll through the document.

Hot tip

Use the Zoom slider located on the bottom of the window frame as an alternative.

150%

Hot tip

The bottom left frame of the window indicates the number of pages and the number of words in the document.

Page: 1 of 1   Words: 310

55

Save the Document

With several lines of text created, save the document currently named the default Document 1, to your hard disk.

1 Click File and select Save. Alternatively, click the Save button on the Quick Access toolbar. The first time you save the file, Word opens the Save As window

2 The Documents library is selected and the first line of the text is suggested as the file name, Desiderata in this case.

3 Accept the library and file names and click Save

4 The Word Titlebar now shows the name of the file, indicating that it has been successfully saved

5 When you next save the file, repeat the same procedure. The existing file will be overwritten with your additions and amendments without further prompting

Save Options

To save the file as a new version with a different name:

1 Click File and select Save As

2 Amend the file name and click Save to create a second copy under the new name

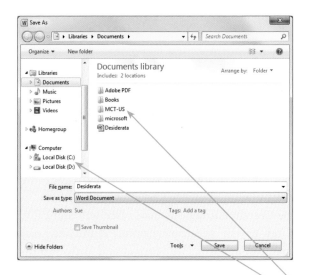

Hot tip

When saving your file, Word will check that you have not already used the file name. If the file already exists, Word will automatically add a sequential number, such as Letter1, Letter2, etc.

You can also change the destination drive or folder:

1 Double-click a different drive or folder in the folder list

2 Alternatively, click New Folder in the Toolbar, name the folder and press Enter to create and open the folder ready to use

To save in a format suitable for users with older versions of Word:

1 Click the Save as type box, and select Word 97-2003 Document (or pick an option like PDF)

2 Name and save the file using the specified format

Hot tip

If you wish to share a file with others who have previous versions of Office, it is essential to save the file as an older version. The default version of an Office 2010 file is unreadable by older applications.

57

Revise the Text

1 If the file is not already open, select File and click Open (or press Ctrl+O)

2 Double-click the file name (or single click and select Open)

Word always opens documents in Insert mode, which means that new text typed between words will be inserted and will automatically push the existing text along.

- Use the Backspace key to remove text to the left of the cursor

- Use the Delete key to delete text to the right of the cursor

- Red wavy lines indicate spelling queries

- Green wavy lines indicate grammar problems

Autocorrect

As you type, certain corrections take place automatically, such as reversal of 'teh' to 'the' and capitalization at the beginning of a new sentence. To view the Autocorrect and Autotype options:

1 Click File, select Options and then Proofing. Click Autocorrect Options to see more details

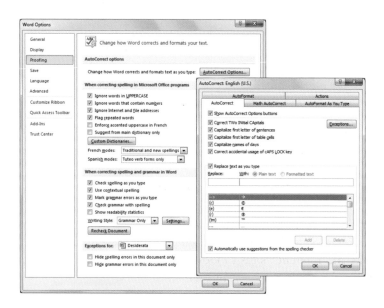

Hot tip

On previous versions of Word, you could switch between Insert mode and Replace mode by pressing the Insert key. To get a similar function in Word 2010, right-click the Status bar and select Overtype.

A button is added to the Status bar, to allow you to switch between Insert and Overtype modes.

Check Spelling

1 Position the cursor anywhere within the text area, choose the Review tab and click Spelling and Grammar

2 The upper pane shows the incorrect spelling in context, with suggestions in the lower pane

3 Click Change to accept the spelling correction or Ignore Once. For technical terms, place names, etc. you might choose Ignore All, or perhaps Add to Dictionary

4 The more subjective Grammar and Style issues offer a similar set of options, or you can clear the Check grammar box and avoid all of them

Proofing and Language Tools

Word 2010 has extensive dictionary and language tools. You can hover over a word and get an instant translation into Arabic, French, Spanish and other languages. The Thesaurus provides alternative words (synonyms and antonyms). The Research option searches reference books and reference sites to locate related information for the selected word.

Move and Copy Text

You can move or copy text within the same document, to another Word document or to another application. Text selected in an application, then cut or copied, is stored by the computer in an area called the Clipboard temporarily.

To copy or move text, you must first select it. You can use any of the following methods:

1 Position the mouse in the left margin, so that it points towards the text. Click to select the line, or keep the mouse button held down and drag down the screen to select more. The text will be highlighted

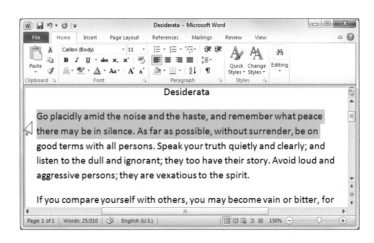

2 Double-click on a single word to select just that word, or triple click to select the paragraph

3 Click at the beginning of the desired text, then press and hold the Shift key and click at the end of the text

4 With the Home tab selected, click Select on the Editing command. This offers further options for more complex actions, such as selecting objects in the background

Don't forget

Double-click in the margin to select the paragraph adjacent to the mouse pointer, or triple-click to select the whole document.

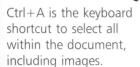
Hot tip

Ctrl+A is the keyboard shortcut to select all within the document, including images.

To Move Text

1 Select the text and click the Cut icon on the Home tab. The text will disappear from the window

2 Position the cursor where you wish to place the text and click the Paste icon

To Copy Text

1 Select the text and click the Copy icon. This time the text will remain in the window

2 Reposition the cursor and click Paste

Office Clipboard

This facility enables you to collect multiple clips and rearrange your document more easily. It holds up to 24 items and can be used to copy text, tables or images within Word or between Office applications, Excel or PowerPointfor example.

To activate the Office Clipboard:

1 Click the small arrow next to Clipboard on the Command bar

2 As you cut or copy a section of text, it will appear in the Clipboard Manager

3 Position the cursor where you wish to paste the text and click on the item. It remains in the clipboard, so you can use it again if needed

4 Click the down arrow on an item and select Delete to remove that item

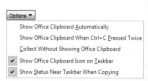

Hot tip

As an alternative, right-click within the highlighted text and, from the Context menu, select Cut or Copy. Reposition the cursor, right-click again and select Paste.

Hot tip

The keyboard shortcuts for these actions are:
Ctrl+X to cut
Ctrl+C to copy
Ctrl+V to paste
These shortcuts work with all the word processors listed on page 52.

Don't forget

Click the Options button to choose whether to show the Office Clipboard automatically.

61

Add Format and Style

Text created in a new Word document is formatted as 'Normal' text. This means that it has specific attributes of font face and size applied by Word. To alter the font:

1 Select the text to change and then, on the Home tab, click the arrow next to the font face or size to choose an option

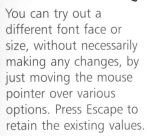
2 Word 2010 has a preview facility that illustrates the effect of the change as you hover over each option in turn

3 The Bold, Italic and Underline tools are toggle switches. Select the text to be formatted and click the required effect. Click again to reverse the action.

Alignment

Text in the document is automatically aligned to the left margin. To change its position:

1 Simply click within the paragraph you wish to realign and click: Left   Center   Right   Justified

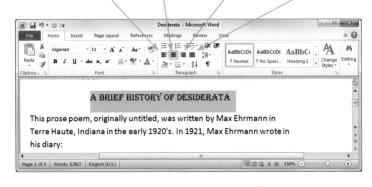

Format Painter

This tool offers a swift way to copy font format, such as font face, size and attributes, including emphasis and alignment.

1 With the Home tab selected, click in the text with the required formatting and then single click the Format Painter tool

2 Move to the target text and click. The format will be applied and the Format Painter released

3 To apply the format to several areas of text, double-click Format Painter and then select each area in turn

4 Single-click Format Painter when finished to release it

Style Options

Word offers a number of style templates. The Normal template is selected when you open the application. To apply a different style:

1 Select all or part of the document and pass your mouse over each of the Quick Style options. The Preview feature will illustrate the effects in turn

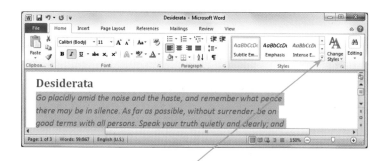

2 Click the up and down arrows to scroll and see further style effects, or click the More button to reveal the full range of options

3 To select a Style, just click on it

Hot tip

Click Change Styles to see an expanded list of style templates, including reverting to Word 2003 or Word 2010 standard styles. Use Change Styles to set the default style for all future documents.

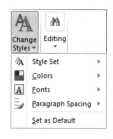

63

Add a Picture

1 Position the cursor where you wish to place the image within the document, inserting a blank line if necessary

When a picture is selected, the Picture Tools Format tab is added. This provides various tools for working with images.

2 Select the Insert tab, and click the Picture button. Locate the image file and click Insert

3 Select the picture, then click the Position button for an instant preview of various positioning effects

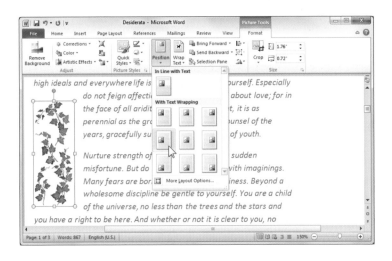

Don't forget

Word has a large range of picture frames and effects that will also give an instant preview.

4 Use the Text Wrapping button for more control of the picture's location. Try options like Square, Tight or Through and drag the picture to the required position

5 To resize the picture, click the up and down buttons on the height. The width will be changed proportionally

6 Click Rotate to flip or rotate the image by 90°, or drag the green Rotation handle for freehand turning

Use Clip Art

Microsoft Office provides a collection of Clip Art images that can be used to illustrate and add interest to your documents.

1 On the Insert tab, click the Clip Art icon to open the Clip Art search

2 Type your keywords, e.g. Peace

3 Specify the results wanted (All Media File types, or a selection from Illustrations, Photographs, Videos and Audio)

4 Click the box to search at Office.com, then click the Go button

5 Scroll through the results to locate a suitable clip

6 Position the cursor where you wish the clip to appear in the document and then click the required image

7 Once inserted, the clip can be repositioned and resized, but be sure to drag one of the corner handles to maintain the correct proportion.

Microsoft Clip Organizer

Select Start, Microsoft Office, Microsoft Office Tools to open the Clip Organizer, which lists all the categories of clips that are stored on your computer and allows you to scroll through and view the full range of images.

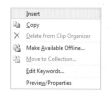

Print the Document

To view the document as it will appear when printed:

1 Select the View tab and click the Print Layout button

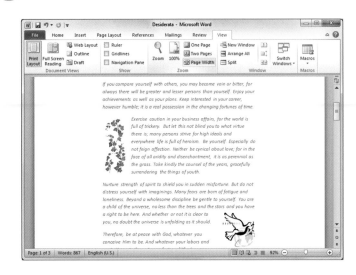

2 Select One Page, Two Pages or Page Width (as shown), or use Zoom for a closer view of a section

3 Select File and then Print to begin the printing process

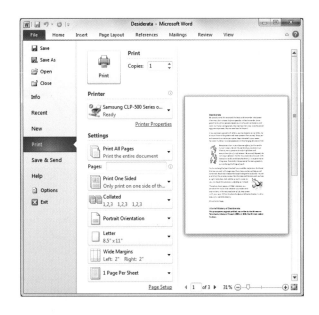

4 Choose the printer to use, if you have more than one available

5 Select Printer Properties to make changes to the settings

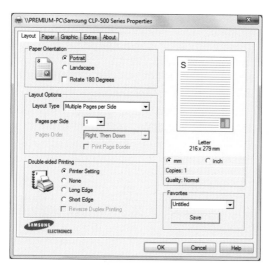

6 Adjust layout and paper size as desired and then click OK

7 Set copies required and click Print

For an immediate print, you can use the Quick Print button. To add this to the Quick Access toolbar:

1 Click the Customize button and choose More Commands

2 Click Quick Print, Add and then click OK

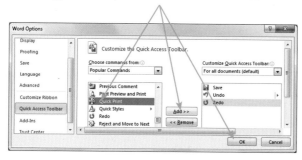

Don't forget

The Quick Print button will print the whole document using the default settings, without the need for pauses and prompts.

Advanced Documents

Microsoft Word offers a whole range of document templates for standard office documents, including letters, faxes and reports. They are displayed in style groups, such as Equity, Median and Oriel. There are also templates for more complicated layouts like brochures, greeting cards and business cards. To view:

1 Click the Office button and select New

2 Installed templates are Microsoft standard, but you can create your own, a letterhead for example, or use those available from Office Online

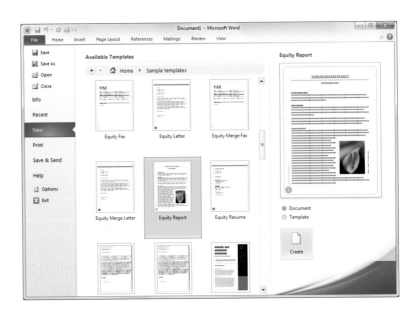

Review, Mailings and References

View the tools and commands on all these tabs within Word to see the extensive range of functions and options you can use to create and manage complex word processor documents.

- Combine reports, track changes and accept or reject amendments with the Review tools

- Use Mail merge to create bulk mailings of letters, envelopes and labels, using criteria to choose recipients

- Use the References tab to help create a composite document with index, table of contents, captions and bibliographies

5 Communication

Communicating with others using your computer is one of its most useful functions. It is more speedy, efficient and cheaper than regular mail. You can contact individuals or whole groups, request receipts to ensure the message has been received, and add automatic signatures. Use Instant Messaging software to chat to people across the world, and a web camera for video.

Email

Email, electronic mail, has the advantage of speed together with the benefits of the written word to support your communication. You can reply to the sender, forward to others and send the same email to whole groups of people. While email has its own conventions, it doesn't have the same formality as regular correspondence.

What you need

Firstly, you need a means to connect to the Internet. This could be a dial-up modem, usually supplied with your computer as a standard component, or a broadband router. This is a separate piece of hardware that is usually broadband supplier specific.

Secondly, you will need an Internet Service Provider (ISP) and ISP account. Your ISP sign-on will provide you with your primary email address, for example:

sue.price14@btinternet.com

Finally, you will need email software. If you are using a dial-up connection, the recommended email software is Windows Live Mail. This application is installed via Windows Live Essentials (see page 27). Earlier versions of Windows included a similar product called Outlook Express. Windows Live Mail allows you to create and read your email off-line, limiting your connection time to the Internet and, therefore, your costs.

With a broadband connection, you can choose to use either Windows Live Mail or web-based email. Most ISPs support both methods of accessing your email account. There are also some email accounts, such as Microsoft Hotmail or Google Gmail, that are particularly designed for Internet access. You access Internet mail using your Internet browser, see page 92.

Windows Live Mail is used for the illustrations and processes in this chapter. However, whichever software you use, Windows Live Mail, another email client application or web-based email, the appearance, facilities and processes are very similar.

Don't forget

The broadband router will connect to your computer via the USB port or Ethernet connection.

Don't forget

You can create and use other email addresses, both for yourself and for other users of your computer. See page 49.

Hot tip

Using Windows Live Mail, your email is stored on your own computer. Web-based mail is stored on the email server and can be accessed from any computer with the correct sign-on.

Create an Account

If you haven't already set up your Internet connection, Windows can help you get started.

1 Select Start, Control Panel, and select Connect to the Internet

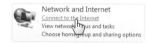

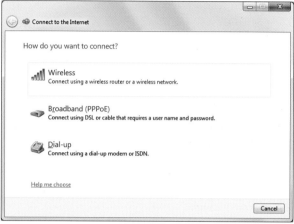

Hot tip

Your chosen ISP may provide a CD, or your computer may have pre-installed software for accessing the Internet and setting up an account.

Don't forget

You can also define your Internet connection via a networked PC or a broadband router.

71

2 Select your connection type - wireless, broadband or dial-up - and follow the prompts to complete the definition

3 Open Windows Live Mail and add your email address and password information and click Next

Hot tip

The first time you start Windows Live Mail, you'll be prompted for your email account details.

4 The connection wizard will locate the appropriate server information, add your email account and set up folders

Receive Email

① 1 Windows Live Mail periodically checks for messages, or you can click Send/Receive to check immediately

② 2 Any messages awaiting you are saved into your Inbox and listed with the sender, subject, date and time

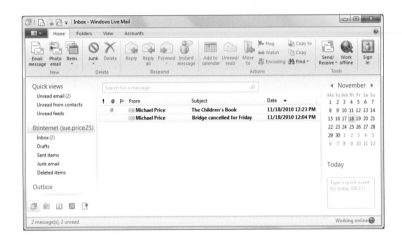

③ 3 Double-click the message title to open and read it. Click the Close button when finished

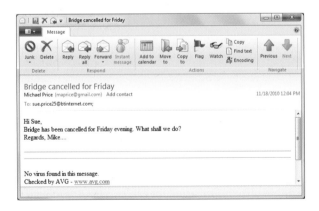

④ 4 Unread messages are indicated by bolder text and an unopened envelope

Hot tip

If you need to connect via your dial-up modem, you will be prompted via a connection window.

Don't forget

In the Folder list, the numbers in brackets, e.g. (2), indicate the number of new/unread messages.

Hot tip

Windows Live Mail has a Reading pane that can show a preview of the selected message. However, for security it is recommended that you turn off this pane.

Reply and Forward

To reply to an incoming email:

1 Select the message from the Inbox and click the Reply button. You can also select Reply from the open message

The address line is automatically completed and Re: is added to the Subject line. The cursor is positioned at the top of the message area, ready for you to type your message.

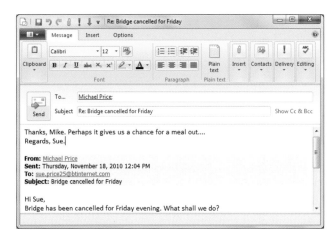

2 Click Send when the response is completed

3 The Inbox entry for the message is modified to show you have replied

!	⁰	⊮	From	Subject	Date ▾
	⁰		Michael Price	The Children's Book	11/18/2010 12:23 PM
			Michael Price	Bridge cancelled for Friday	11/18/2010 12:04 PM

4 Use Reply All rather than Reply to respond to all the people who received the original message

5 To send the message on to other recipients, select or open the message and click Forward. This time Fw: is added to the Subject line and you can add the email addresses for the To:, Cc: or Bcc: fields (see page 74)

Don't forget

The text of the original message is appended to the reply, which ensures that both correspondents are aware of the details.

Hot tip

When you send an email, it is saved in your Outbox where it will then be sent on to the recipients.

Don't forget

When using Reply, any attachments will be stripped from the email. If you Forward the message, then the attachments remain. See page 76 for working with attachments.

Send Email

1 From the Inbox, click the Create Mail button to open the New Message window

2 Start typing the recipient's name or email address in the To: field, matching entries from your Contacts list (see page 78) will be displayed

(see page 78)

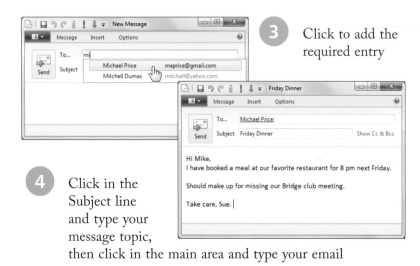

3 Click to add the required entry

4 Click in the Subject line and type your message topic, then click in the main area and type your email

5 Click Show Cc & Bcc to send copies to others

6 When finished click the Send button

The message will be moved to your Outbox, which will then indicate the number of messages waiting to be sent.

Messages will stay in the Outbox until you click on Send/Receive, or until your system does an automatic Send/Receive

A copy of the email is saved in your Sent Items folder

Email Options

To control the Send and Receive functions on your email account:

1 Open Windows Live Mail, click the application icon and select Options, Mail, then click the General tab

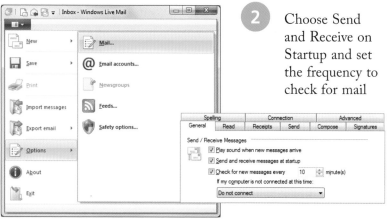

2 Choose Send and Receive on Startup and set the frequency to check for mail

3 Click the Read tab and tick the box to Read all messages in plain text. This is the preferred option for greater security

4 On the Send tab, you can see a whole range of features that enable you to customize Windows Mail to your personal requirements

5 Select Signatures to specify the signature you want applied to all outgoing messages

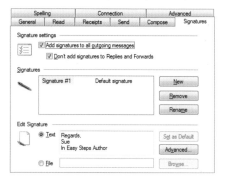

Don't forget

Email text can be plain text or Rich text (html). It's a good idea to choose to send mail in plain text. Many companies are wary of email containing formatted text and will block them from their systems.

Sending and receiving in plain text will prevent the embedding of attached pictures within the message. Use Rich text when you need to send tables or other such data.

Hot tip

Replying to messages in the format they were sent is the polite option.

Attachments

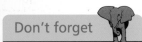

Hot tip

An attachment is a file created outside of the email program. It could be in one of many formats, such as a photograph, text document, spreadsheet or scanned document.

Don't forget

You should be aware of the size of the file when sending attachments. It will be indicated in the Attach line of the header. Large files, photograph files in particular, can take a long time to send and/or be received on a dial-up connection. Some photo programs, such as Microsoft's Photo Premium 10, have a facility that will reduce the file size for emailing as an attachment.

To send an attachment with your email:

1 Create your email message, then click the Attach button

2 The Documents library opens, for you to locate the required folder and file

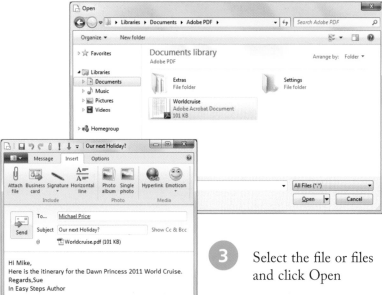

3 Select the file or files and click Open

4 The message will display the details of the attached file(s)

5 Click Send and the message is added to the Outbox

When you receive an email with one or more attachments:

1 The Inbox entry for the message has a Paperclip symbol

2 Open the message to see details of the attachment(s)

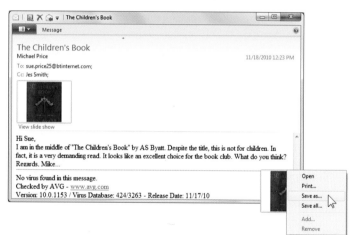

3 Click the attachment icon to view it, or right-click to select Save As (or Save all, for multiple attachments)

4 The attachment will be saved in the Documents library by default, but you can select a different folder

5 To open the attachment in its associated application, double-click the file icon

Contacts

Your Windows Live Mail Contacts list acts as your address book and can be used to hold a wide range of details about family, friends and businesses. Details like work address, birthdays and anniversaries, as well as the usual home address, email and phone numbers can be stored.

To view the Contacts list:

1 Open Windows Live Mail and select the Contacts shortcut

2 The contact names are listed, along with brief details for the selected contact

3 Click the New Contact button and fill in the Quick add name, and email fields, plus phone or company, if known

4 When the details have been entered, click the Add Contact button and the new contact will appear in the list

Other methods of adding contacts to your Contacts folder include:

1 Right-click an email in the Inbox list and select Add sender to contacts

2 Open a message, right-click an email address (sender or recipient), then choose Add to Contacts

3 Open Mail Options (see page 75) and select the Send tab, then ensure you have selected Automatically put people I reply to in my address book after the third reply

You can use the Contacts list to create a new email message:

1 Locate the contact and select the name, then single-click the appropriate email address from the contact details

2 This opens a new message window with the To: box already filled in

(see page 75)

Don't forget

If the email is already in the Contacts list, Add sender to contacts is greyed (unavailable) and Add to contacts changes to Edit Contacts.

Hot tip

To make it easier to search the Contact lists, you can select Sort by and choose either First name or Last name, as you prefer.

79

Hot tip

You can also right-click a contact name, select Send Email and then choose an email address for that person.

Contact Category

Creating a category of contacts makes it easier to communicate with a selection of your contacts. You send the email to all the contacts in that category in one easy step, without having to address them individually. To create a Contact Category:

1 Display the Contacts list and click the Category button in the Home, New area

2 Supply a category name and then click the contacts you want, one by one, to add them to the box

3 When you have added all the contacts for that category, click Save

4 The categories are listed in alphabetical order, along with All Contacts

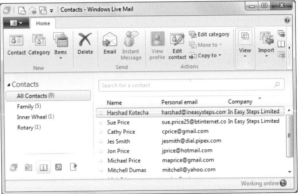
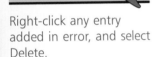

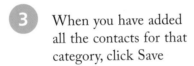

5 Select any category to see its contents

6 Use category names to address messages just like email ids

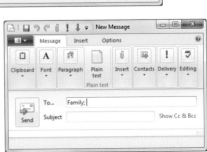

80

Manage Your Email

Windows Live Mail is structured with a series of folders to contain and organize your mail.

- Inbox is where your mail arrives and is usually stored

- Outbox holds the messages you create until you initiate Send and Receive

- Sent items contains a copy of all messages sent

- Deleted items stores messages that you no longer want

- Drafts contains email messages that you wish to complete and send later

- Junk mail holds items that either you or Windows Live Mail considers to be unwanted or unsolicited messages

You can create your own folders to organize your mail:

1. Right-click the Inbox and select New Folder

2. Name the new folder, confirm the containing folder, then click OK

3. The new folder is added in its assigned location

4. Drag and drop mail from the Inbox to the new folder

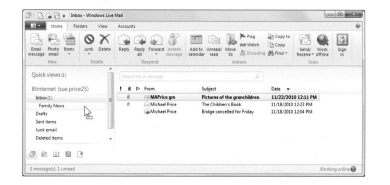

Hot tip

The Junk mail folder may be called Bulk mail in web-based email.

Hot tip

Another option when you have many emails is to sort the items within the folder. Click a header label (e.g. From or Date), to sort by that field. A second click on the header label will reverse the order.

Junk Email

Junk email, or spam, is the computerized equivalent of the unsolicited mail that comes through your door every day. Most ISPs provide filters that will try to eliminate or redirect spam so that it doesn't actually reach your computer. Your antivirus program may redirect suspect mail. Windows Live Mail lets you set up your own rules to block suspect senders and to redirect any junk mail that may get through.

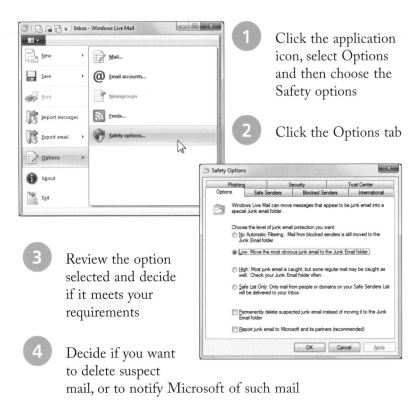

1 Click the application icon, select Options and then choose the Safety options

2 Click the Options tab

3 Review the option selected and decide if it meets your requirements

4 Decide if you want to delete suspect mail, or to notify Microsoft of such mail

5 Click the Safe Senders and Blocked Senders tabs in turn and add any specific email addresses or domain names

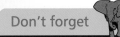
6 Click the Phishing tab and you'll see that Windows Live Mail protects your Inbox from phishing attacks

82

Sometimes messages may be incorrectly classified, but you do have the facility to reclassify them manually:

1. Right-click an Inbox spam message and select Junk e-mail, then choose an action, such as Mark as junk

2. For a message that has been incorrectly directed to the Junk folder, you have the option to Mark as not junk

If you use PC based mail, you should check online from time to time, check to see if any valid or expected email has been trapped by your ISP. For example:

1. Connect to the Internet and sign in to your account to view your mail at the server

2. Select the Bulk or Spam folder, and review the contents to identify those that should not be treated as spam

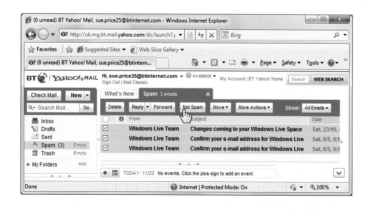

3. Select the messages, move them to the Inbox and sign out. Windows Live Mail will download those messages

Email Hints and Tips

1 You may receive email messages from banks and other organizations you conduct business with. The message will usually contain information about your account and inform you that you cannot use this address for correspondence, for example:

NoReply-FlyingBlue@airfrance.fr

These messages are automatically generated and are not monitored email addresses

2 Occasionally, an email you send may fail to arrive. There are several causes. It may be that you typed an incorrect email address, or the contact's server was off-line or busy. In these cases, you will usually receive an error message.

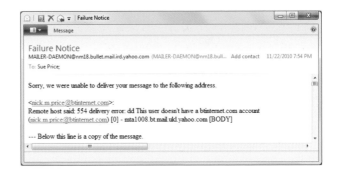

Check the email address and, if that is correct, just try again later, when the server may be back in service

3 With important messages, you can add a priority flag to attract the attention of the recipient, so the message isn't just missed

4 For more certainty, you can add a Read Receipt to the message. When the recipient opens the message, you will be notified

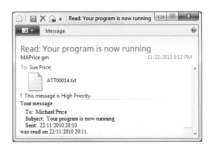

5 Some emails, newsletters for example, have images stored at a website. For security, these pictures are blocked. Only download them if you recognize and trust the website

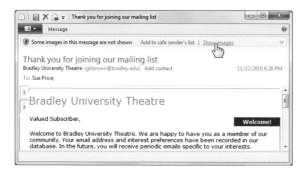

6 When you subscribe to newsletters, you'll usually find an Update or Unsubscribe link at the end of each newsletter

7 Select Options, Mail, Compose, and Mail Font Settings

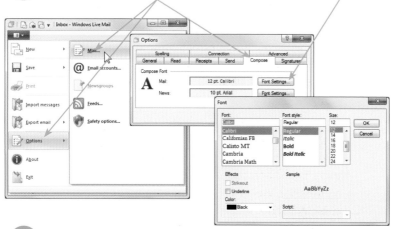

8 Click OK to apply changes

Hot tip

Most ISPs allow you to have more than one email address. Use a different address for subscribing to Internet sites, to protect your main address.

Beware

With email messages that are unsolicited or from a dubious website, avoid unsubscribing as this will actually validate your email address with the spammer.

Hot tip

You can select the font type, style and size, plus effects like underline and color.

Newsgroups

A newsgroup is a discussion group on the Internet, open to all and centered around a mutual interest or topic. Newsgroups can be a valuable source of help and information on topics as wide ranging as Archeology to Zoology, Terry Pratchett to rocket maintenance. The newsgroup community is important to many participants, it means that they can discuss their interest with those of a like mind.

To be able to participate, you need to use a program like Windows Live Mail to communicate with a newsgroup server managing collections of newsgroup. You subscribe to a particular newsgroup, where you'll see questions and answers and follow threads of related posts from other members. Similarly, when you post a message or reply, everyone can see your comments.

To specify the newsgroup server to Windows Live Mail:

1. Select the Accounts tab and click Newsgroup in the New Account section

2. Supply the display name or nickname that you want others to see and click Next

3. Provide your email address for personal replies

You could make a deliberate error, to avoid it being detected by robots

4 Name the newsgroup server you have decided to use, for example: freenews.netfront.net

Hot tip

This is a free news server and has no log on. If you sign up for a paid service, you'd be given a user ID and password.

5 Click Next, then click Finish to add the account

6 The list of newsgroups will be downloaded, well over 40,000 are listed in this case.

Hot tip

Newsgroup Netiquette is basic etiquette for posting messages and replies. Many sites will give you guidelines for best practice. Good sites are well monitored and moderated.

7 Type one or more keywords to list newsgroups that are relevant to your particular interests, e.g. Bridge

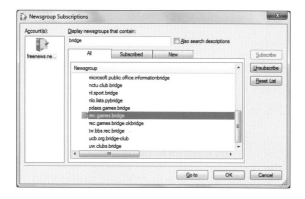

Hot tip

When you have reviewed the newsgroup (see page 88), you can choose Unsubscribe if you do not wish to receive any future postings from that newsgroup.

8 Select a specific newsgroup, click Subscribe and Go to

87

Review the Newsgroup

When you subscribe to a newsgroup, the recent posts are downloaded, and new posts will be downloaded when they are added to the server.

1 Click the ▷ next to a post to expand the conversation (and the ◢ to collapse the associated set of posts)

View Layout provides the option to display a preview of the selected post in the Reading Pane, below or to the right of the message list. However, for security, this is best avoided.

2 Double-click a post to review the contents, and follow posts in turn to see the flow of the conversation

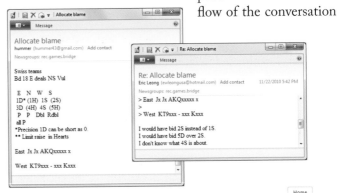

You may find that the sender has modified the email address to foil spammers. In that case, you'll need to amend the address before sending.

3 Select a post and choose Reply to respond to the sender only, or select Reply to group, to let everyone see your comments

Instant Messaging

The ID you set up for Windows Live Mail can also be used to communicate with others live, using the instant messaging application Windows Live Messenger. You can download this as part of Windows Live Essentials (see page 27) or as a single program at http://explore.live.com/windows-live-messenger.

Hot tip

Hot tip

The Download Now link on either web page allows you to download and install the whole of Windows Live Essentials, or a selected subset.

1 Click Download Now, to select and install Messenger and any other Windows Live programs that you may want

2 The first time you start Windows Live Messenger, you will be asked for your Windows Live ID (see page 71)

Don't forget

You can link to many services, such as games, music, photos, shopping, travel and videos, as well as social networking.

3 You can choose to sign in at start up, link to services, such as Facebook, and add your cell phone number, as desired

...cont'd

4 Choose your privacy setting - Public, Limited or Private - to control who has access to your details and activities

5 Click Add a contact, then specify the email address

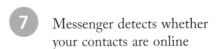

6 An invitation is sent as an email or as an instant message if the contact is online

7 Messenger detects whether your contacts are online

8 To start a conversation, double-click a name, or just press Enter to work with the selected name

6 Surfing the Internet

The Internet is an enormous resource, so you need to find your way around using web addresses and using search engines to locate websites and web pages of interest. Internet Explorer helps, with tabbed browsing and with favorites and history. You can choose a home page, save pages of interest and print web pages. As you get used to the Internet, you can move on to cost effective shopping, investing and banking online.

What's Needed

Don't forget

Internet Explorer is the Internet browser that is provided with Windows 7 by default. Other Internet browsers include Mozilla, Firefox and Opera.

The requirements for accessing websites on the Internet are similar to those for electronic mail communications (see page 70):

● Computer with Internet connection
● Account with an Internet Service Provider (ISP)

In addition, you will require:

● Internet browser software, such as Internet Explorer
● Antivirus software and other security add-ins

To start Internet Explorer:

1 Click the browser shortcut on the taskbar, or select Start, All Programs and then Internet Explorer

Hot tip

For an alternative shortcut, right-click the Start menu entry for Internet Explorer and choose Pin to Start Menu, to add it to the top level.

2 The browser will open and display the default startup web page, http://www.msn.com in this example

The default startup web page is known as your Home Page. It is initially assigned by Windows or by your computer supplier, but you can choose any web page you wish to act as your home page (see page 107).

3 To view a web page, click in the address bar area, type the address, e.g. www.nationalgeographic.com, and press Enter

4 The requested web page is displayed. Click one of the links to switch to a related web page, for example <u>Maps</u> which displays www.nationalgeographic.com/maps

Web Addresses

The full web page address for National Geographic maps is:

http://nga.nationalgeographic.com/maps/index.html

This address is also known as a URL (universal resource locator) and it contains the following parts:

http://	Hypertext Transfer Protocol (protocol used for transferring web pages)
nga.nationalgeographic.com	host name of computer
maps	Directory structure (one or more folders)
index.html	File name of web page

The host name of the computer ends with an extension that usually indicates the type of institution. The values can include:

.com commercial institution

.net commercial institution (addition to .com)

.edu educational institution

.org not-for-profit organization

.gov government institution

.mil military

The extension may also indicate the country where the institution is located, for example:

.at	Austria
.au	Australia
.ca	Canada
.uk	United Kingdom

If no web page name is provided, the browser will look for a default name, trying a variety of names including:

default.htm	default.asp	index.php
index.html	index.htm	index.shtml

Search for Web Pages

If you aren't sure of the exact web page address, or are just interested to find useful pages, you can use the Instant Search Box.

1 Click the search box, type a relevant word or phrase, **night sky** for example, and then press Enter

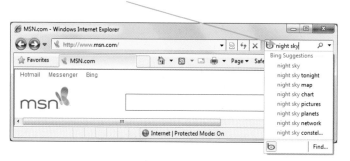

2 Links to the first ten web pages are listed, along with the total number of matches – in this case over 71 million

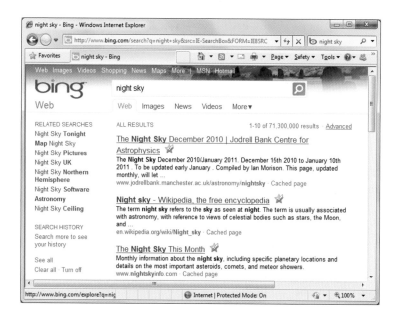

3 Select a suitable web page from the results displayed, or scroll down and select another set of ten

Hot tip

By default, Internet Explorer uses Microsoft's Bing search, but you can change the search provider (see page 96).

Don't forget

You can switch to lists of Images, Videos, Shopping, News, Maps or other categories, all based on the same search text as the web page list.

Hot tip

You may be offered a list of related searches, and there may be several Sponsored sites that have paid a fee to be positioned prominently on the results page.

Change Search Provider

You can have different search providers in addition to or in place of the Microsoft Bing Search default.

1 Click the arrow at the right of the Instant Search Box and choose Find More Providers

2 Select a search provider, click Make this my default search provider, if desired, then click Add Provider

3 Click the Search Box arrow again to select a provider to use for the remainder of the Internet Explorer session (or until the next change)

Page Back and Forward

When you view new web pages, your browser remembers the pages you have already visited.

1 Click the back arrow to go back to the previous page

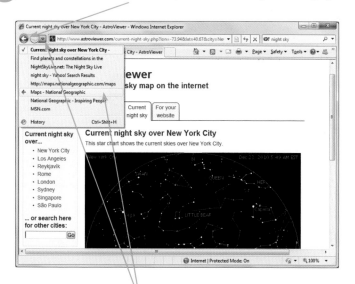

Don't forget

Click the Back icon to display the immediately previous page. When you view a previous page, the Forward icon is enabled and will display the next page in the sequence.

2 Click the down arrow to list all the pages you've viewed, and click any entry to switch to that place in the sequence

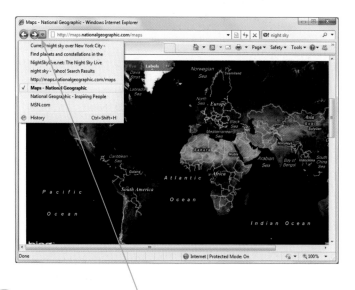

Beware

If you select any link on one of the previous pages, the record from that point on will be discarded and replaced by the newly selected page, unless you use a new window or new tab (see page 98).

3 Click the down arrow again to select a different page

Open New Window

You can open a new browser window, to avoid discarding an existing sequence of pages. The options include:

1 Select the Internet Explorer icon from the Start menu or Launch bar to open a separate copy at the Home page

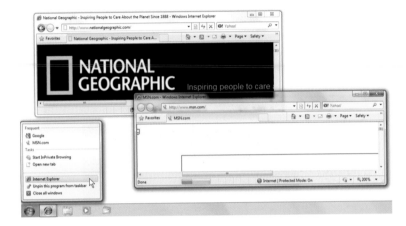

2 Right-click the required link and select Open in New Window to display that web page

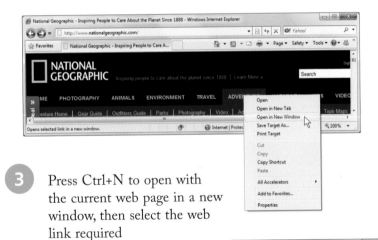

3 Press Ctrl+N to open with the current web page in a new window, then select the web link required

4 Press Ctrl+O and specify the web page address to open that page in a new window

Use Tabbed Browsing

With Internet Explorer 7.0 and later versions, you have the option to use tabs to display multiple web pages in the same window.

1 Type a web page address and press Alt+Enter to open the page on a separate tab and make it the foreground tab

2 Right-click a hyperlink and select Open in New Tab

3 Type keywords in the search box and press Alt+Enter to carry out the search and display the results on a new tab

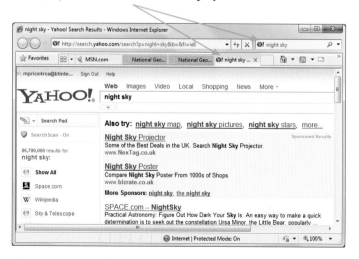

Don't forget

To open a new blank tab, click the New Tab button (or press Ctrl+T).

Hot tip

You can also press Ctrl then left-click the link. In either case, the current tab remains in the foreground. Press Ctrl+Shift and click the link to make it become the foreground.

Don't forget

Click any tab to switch that tab to foreground, or press Ctrl+n where n is tab number 1-8. Ctrl+9 selects the last tab, however many tabs there are.

Quick Tabs

When you have more than one tab in use, the Quick Tabs button appears to the left of the row of tabs.

 1   Click the down arrow next to the Quick Tabs button to display the full names of the web pages on the tabs

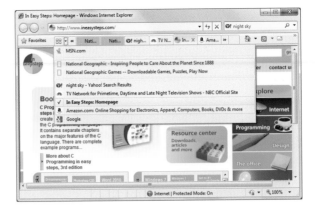

2   Click any web page title to make that tab the foreground

3   Click the Quick Tabs button itself to display miniature thumbnails of the pages, to help select the required one

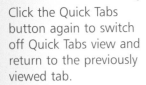
4   Click a web page thumbnail to view it, or click the ☒ at the top right of the thumbnail to close that tab

1 To close a tab from the tab row, click the tab to bring it to the foreground, then click the  that appears

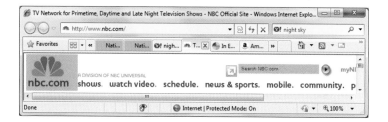

Don't forget

With only one tab in effect, clicking the Close button ends Internet Explorer without any interaction.

2 To close all the tabs at once, click the  symbol on the main window

3 Select Close all tabs, or you can click Close current tab

The next time you start the browser, you can re-open the same set of tabs you had when you closed the previous session.

Hot tip

If you change your mind about closing all the tabs, click the Close button on this message to cancel the operation.

101

1 Select the New Tab button, and choose to Reopen Last Browsing Session

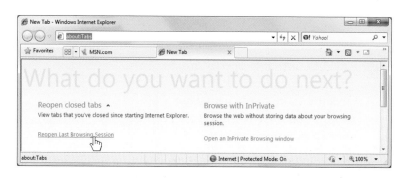

View Details

Web pages can be filled with lots of information, and sometimes use small text sizes to fit everything onto the page. There are several ways to make things easier to see:

1 Click Page, then click Text Size, where Medium is the default, and choose your preferred size

Only the text components of the web page will be scaled. The graphics and images are not resized. To adjust the scale for all the components of the web page:

2 Click the arrow next to the Zoom button and select the scale you want to try

3 Select Custom to specify an exact scale between 10% and 1000%. Note that scale factors below 100% are useful for web page overviews

4 Click the Zoom button to reset the scaling to 100%

...cont'd

Internet Explorer has particular support for large images.

1 Click on the image of the Taj Mahal at Wikipedia

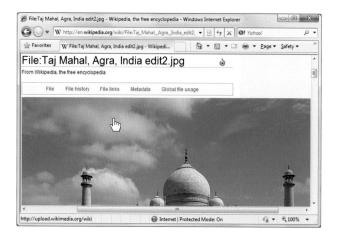

Hot tip

This page contains a 800 x 526 preview image, which promises a larger 3840 x 2525 jpeg image.

2 What's displayed is a small image that shows the whole of the picture. Note the Magnify cursor

3 Click on the image to expand it

Don't forget

When the picture is too large to fit in the window area, it is initially displayed in a reduced size to fit.

103

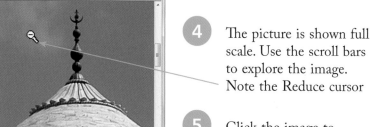

4 The picture is shown full scale. Use the scroll bars to explore the image. Note the Reduce cursor

5 Click the image to display the complete image once again

Web Address Reminder

The addresses are shown in the sequence they were typed, with the newest addresses at the top. Use the scroll bar to view more addresses.

When you want to repeat a web address that you've visited previously, Internet Explorer can remind you of the full address.

1 Click the down arrow at the end of the address bar and select an address from those you've typed previously

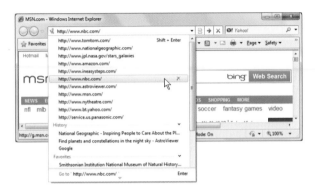

Matching alternatives appear as you type. The one you want appears when you've typed enough to identify it.

2 Type the first part of the address, and select the full web page address when it appears

You can also use the Instant Search box (see page 42) or carry out a search from the Address bar.

For clarity, you can prefix the search text with the command Find, Go or ? when you enter a search on the address bar.

3 Type appropriate keywords or page name and press Enter, or press Alt+Enter to display the results on a new tab

Favorites Center

Internet Explorer keeps a note of all the websites and web pages you visit. To review your browsing history:

1 Click the Favorites button, then select the History tab in the Favorites Center

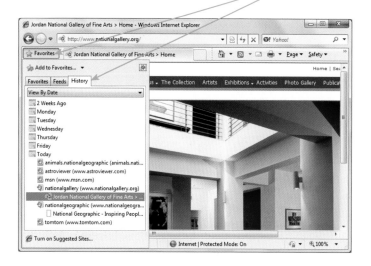

Don't forget

The Favorites Center includes web page Favorites (see page 106), RSS Feeds (see page 134) and the browsing History, as discussed on this page.

2 Click a day or week to expand the contents. Click a website entry to show the web pages viewed

3 Select a web page to view its contents. This removes the History list from view

4 To change the sequence in which the History is displayed, click the arrow next to the View By button and choose By Date, By Site, By Most Visited, or By Order Visited Today

Hot tip

To keep the list you'd click , which turns to an [X] and the Favorites Center will be pinned to the window.

5 Choose Search History and type appropriate keywords, then click Search Now to list the web pages that have those keywords included in their titles

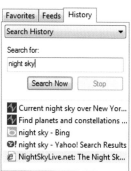

...cont'd

When you find a web page that you know you'll want to visit again, you can add it to your Favorites list.

1 While viewing the web page, click the Favorites button, and then click Add to Favorites

2 Amend the page name, if desired

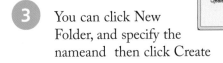

3 You can click New Folder, and specify the nameand then click Create

4 Click Add to put the web page reference in the specified folder

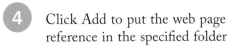

5 To use the shortcuts, click the Favorites button and then click the Favorites tab

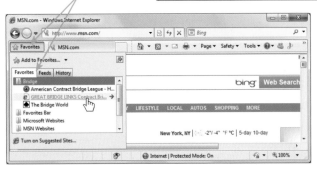

Home Pages

If there's a page you'd always want to start off with, you can make it your home page or add it to your set of home page tabs.

1 Visit the web page, **www.google.com** for example

Don't forget

When you change your home page or home page tabs, you can save the results as a Favorite web page or Favorite tab group, so you can easily restore your home page settings in the future.

2 Click the arrow next to the Home button and select Add or Change Home Page

3 Choose the appropriate option

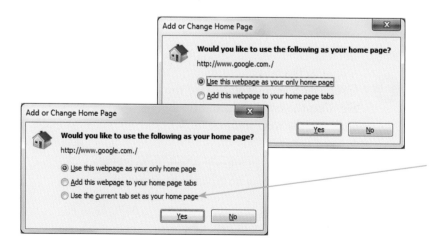

Beware

There is a third option, Use the Current Tab Set as your Home Page, that is offered when you have two or more tabs open in Internet Explorer.

4 Click Yes to save your changes

Save Web Page

Another way to make sure you can always access the contents of a particular web page is to save it on your hard disk.

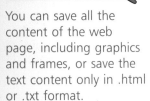
1 With the web page displayed, click the Page button and select the Save As entry from the list

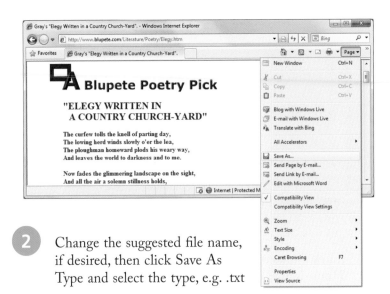

2 Change the suggested file name, if desired, then click Save As Type and select the type, e.g. .txt

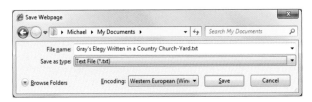

3 Click the Save button to save the file onto the hard disk, and double-click the file icon to open in Notepad

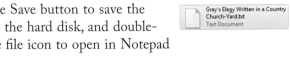

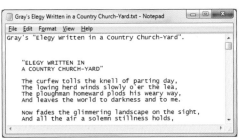

You can let others know about web pages you find interesting.

1 Open the web page in Internet Explorer and click Page

2 Select Send Page by Email to send the actual content of the web page in an email message

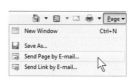

3 Select Send Link by Email to create an email message with the web page address (URL), ready for you to complete and send

Print Web Page

1 To see how the current web page will print, click the arrow next to the Print button and select Print Preview

Click the arrow next to the Print Size box to pick a scale value between 30% and 200%. Click Custom to see the value set for Shrink to Fit, or to set a specific value.

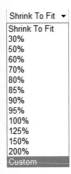

Choosing a higher scale value may result in parts of the web page being truncated during print.

2 By default, Internet Explorer will shrink the page to fit the paper, using a scale value of 78% in this case

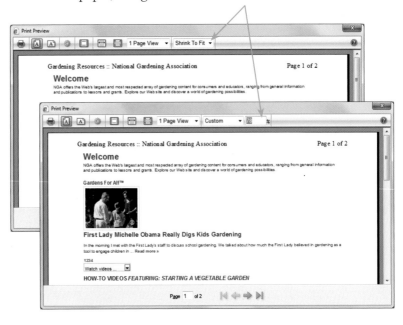

3 Click the Print Document button to send the web page to the printer, or press Esc to end the print preview

Shopping on the Internet

1   To see a typical shopping website, visit www.amazon.com

Don't forget

One of the great benefits of the Internet is shopping. You can use websites to help you identify the best products and where to find them. Often, you'll get the best prices by completing the purchase at a website.

2   Click Start Here, enter your email ID and click Sign In

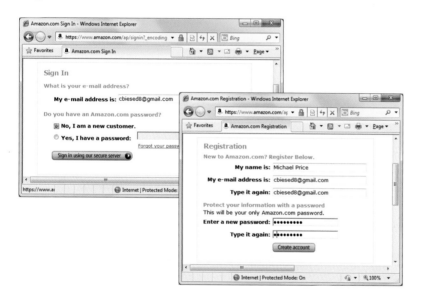

Beware

If you visit Amazon. com from a region other than the USA, you'll be advised to switch to the local Amazon website.

Shopping from the UK?
Visit
amazon.co.uk
▸ Shop now

Hot tip

All that's needed to register at the Amazon website is your name, your email address and a password.

3   Now you can explore and search the website for books, etc.

Hot tip

Choose a department, such as Books or Cameras or Computers, and browse the products or type a search keyword to find specific items.

...cont'd

4 Amazon remembers the products you review, and will make recommendations based on your browsing history

5 When you've found something you want, click Add to Cart. A summary of your shopping cart is displayed

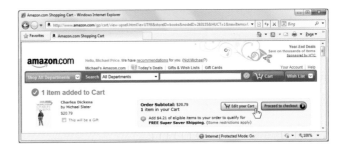

6 Click Edit Shopping Cart to change the quantities or to remove unwanted items

7 Search for more items to add to your shopping cart (or add to your wish list as a reminder for later)

To display and edit the contents of your shopping cart or wish list at any time, click the appropriate icon at the top of the page.

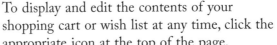

Place Your Order

1 Click the Proceed to Checkout button, and sign in with email ID and password

2 Enter the shipping address, choose a shipping option, then select the payment method that suits you

3 Review your order and click Place Your Order to confirm

Don't forget

Adding an item to your shopping cart doesn't reserve the item, and there's no commitment to purchase until you actually place your order.

Beware

If you register at the USA site but are located overseas, your orders will be sent by international shipping. It's much better to register and place orders at your local Amazon website.

113

Hot tip

Amazon offers a variety of payment methods, including credit card, store card, checking account, money order and an option to be billed for the order.

Don't forget

The progress bar shows the steps for preparing and submitting your order. The final step commits you to the purchase.

Money Management

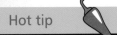
114

1 Visit **finance.yahoo.com** and click a tab, such as Investing

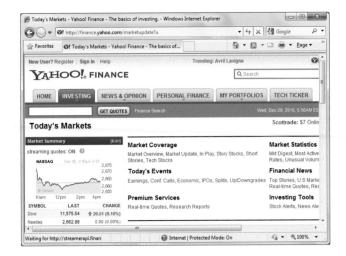

2 You can participate in online banking, which will give you 24/7 access to your checking and savings accounts

3 The address bar background shows the security status:

Red	–	Out of date or invalid
Yellow	–	Unverified
White	–	Normal validation
Green	–	Extended validation

Only provide personal information on fully secure sites

7 Personal Internet

Make the Internet personal for you. You can create and manage your own website, starting with a free service then moving on to your own domain. Set up a blog or web diary on your website, or on a specialized service. Participate in a social network or take advantage of web feeds. You can even explore your family tree.

Create a Website

Perhaps the best way to understand the Internet is to create your own website. It isn't as difficult as you might think, and it needn't be expensive. In fact, we can start off with a completely free website, just to get a feel for what might be involved and whether it might be something worth pursuing more seriously.

You'll need a name for your website, an associated email address, somewhere to store your web pages (the website host) and facilities for creating and updating web pages. For our example website, we'll use one of the free website host services.

1   Visit the website www.webs.com and click Start Now

2   Provide the details requested to create your account

3   Specify your desired site name, which forms part of the website address, and provide the site title and category

4 Scroll down to the next section and select a template for your site, Clean Splash for example

Don't forget

There are over 300 templates available, and you can change your selection at any time if you wish.

5 Check the box to agree to the terms of service and then click Next Step

6 Accept or amend the recommended pages for your site, choose additional pages, if desired, then click Create My Site

7 Select the Webs package you want (Basic, Enhanced or Pro) or click Continue for the standard free package

Hot tip

The alternative packages are fee-based and they provide extra features and support, and avoid the ads (see page 121) that cover the cost of the free facilities.

Build the Website

1 Webs Site Builder opens, ready to create the Home page

2 Click Content Box to begin adding text and images

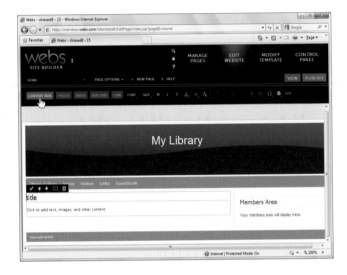

3 Enter the title and text or images required. Click the Tick on the toolbar to confirm

4 Click Publish to save changes to the page

5 Click View to see the page as it appears in the browser - complete with ads

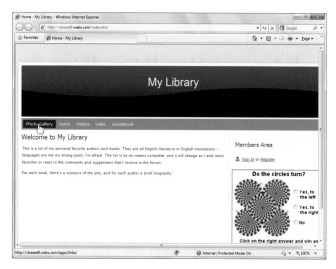

6 Close the browser window to return to the edit session and select a page to edit, the Photo Gallery for example

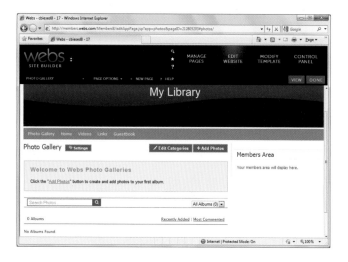

7 Click Add Photos to create an album and insert photos and pictures into it (see page 120)

119

Add Photos to an Album

1 When you select Add Photos, you can name your first album and then select Upload Photos to choose images

2 The Documents library is displayed, and you can navigate to the required folder and select the image you want

3 Click Upload Photos to add more images, then click Submit to add all the photos to your album

4 Edit and reorder the photos in your new album, as desired

5 Scroll down and select Save to store the album and its images

6 Select View to see the album and other pages of the website in your browser

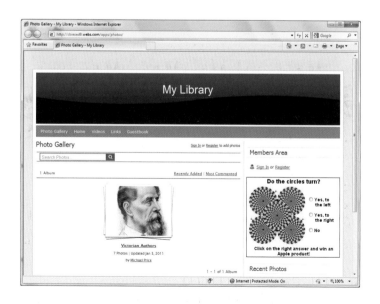

Add a Page

1 Click the Add New Page button to select the type of page required

Hot tip

You can add all the pages needed and build their content later, or create each page as you go along.

Hot tip

The Page Name is used to create the page address in the form: siteaddress.webs.com/ pagename.htm (uses lower case, removes spaces and adds .htm). The page name is added to the navigation bar.

Don't forget

When you Publish the changes, they will be available to anyone who has the address and views your website.

2 Choose page type (blank or predefined) and specify the page name, e.g. Charles Dickens, to create a web page with the address cbiesed8.webs.com/charlesdickens.htm

3 Click the Content Box to add title and text or images

4 Select Publish to save your new page, then add and publish any other pages, Jane Austen for example

5 To remove the navigation bar entry, select Manage Pages

Hot tip

If you will be creating a growing list of pages, for authors or for books for example, you may find them easier to manage with a separate Links page (see page 124).

6 Click the Visible icon for each of the pages that you want to hide, and confirm the changes you make

Don't forget

When you select Manage Pages, you can also edit, view, protect or delete pages, and add new pages to the website.

7 The selected pages are removed from the navigation bar, but are retained as part of the website

Add Links to Website

1 While editing the website, select the Links page and click the Add Links button

2 Specify a Category, provide the web page URL, page name (and description, if required) and click Submit

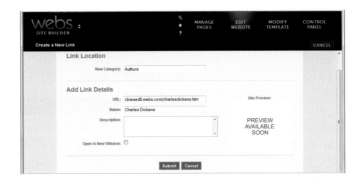

3 The category is created and the page link is inserted, and a preview of the page is displayed

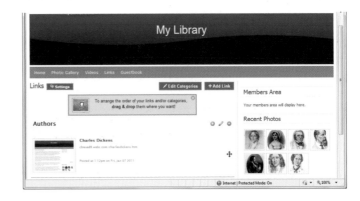

4 View your website and select the Links page to see categories and pages that have been added

You can also put links onto individual pages in your website. For example, to add book synopsis links at the bottom of an Author page:

Hot tip

The preview picture and the page name are hyperlinks to the page addressed by the URL shown.

1 Edit the author page, then add a contents box and provide the title, Books for example

2 Enter a book title in the text section, highlight it and click the Link button

Don't forget

You can also insert links to other websites, email addresses, paragraphs on the current page or files on your website.

3 Click My Pages, choose the required page and click Insert Link

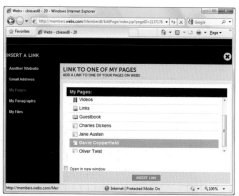

4 The selected text becomes a hyperlink

Blogging

A blog (short for web log) is a website with regular journal style entries, such as event descriptions or comments. The entries are usually text but they may include pictures, videos and links to other blogs or web pages. Blogs can be personal or corporate, and may be individual websites or hosted on a specialized server. To create a website blog using your Webs.com website:

1 Open www.webs.com, sign in to your website and select Manage Pages and Add a New Page

2 Choose the Blog page type, revise the page name, if necessary, and click Create Page

3 You can now set up your blog and start adding entries

4 Select Settings to control how your blog operates

5 Select Edit Categories to add terms to arrange blog entries

6 Select Post New Entry, and add title, categories and text

Hot tip

You can provide a description for the blog, say who can add entries and add comments, and specify if approval is required before members comments are displayed.

Don't forget

Categories give you ways to access subsets of the messages that are posted to your blog.

Hot tip

When you Publish an entry, the counts for the associated categories will be incremented.

View Blog

1 Visitors to your website can select the Blog page and view all the entries, in full or summary

2 Visitors may add comments to any entry in the blog

Now you can change the permissions for any member, to Moderator for example.

3 The website owner and moderators can edit or delete any post, including comments made by visitors

Blogging Service

1 Visit www.blogger.com, specify your Google account email address and password, and click Sign In

Don't forget

You don't have to create a complete website if all you want is a blog page. You can use a dedicated blogging service, such as Blogger.com from Google. If you don't have a Google account, select Get Started to create one.

Don't have a Google Account?
Get started

2 Specify your name and display name, accept the terms and conditions and click Continue

3 Type the title and the name to use for your first blog and then click Continue

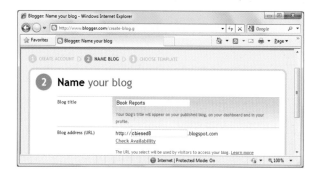

Hot tip

The name is used as part of the URL for your blog. Click the link to Check Availability in case your preferred name is already allocated.

http://cbiesed8.blogspot.com
Check Availability
This blog address is available.

...cont'd

4 Select a template to apply to your blog. Your selection can be changed later if you wish

5 When the blog has been created, click Start Blogging

6 Enter the title and the text for your first entry, then click Publish Post to make it ready for viewing on the web

Social Networking

You can use the Internet to help keep in touch with friends and others with shared interests. Popular sites include MySpace, YouTube, Twitter and Facebook. Originally, these were the preserve of the 18 to 24 age group, these sites have now been opened up for anyone to join, businesses and political parties included. To join Twitter:

1 Go to **www.twitter.com** and click the Sign Up button

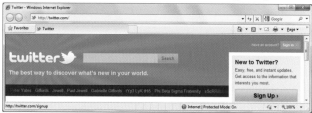

2 Provide your name, username, password and email address and click the button to Create my account

Don't forget

You must respond to the message from Twitter to confirm your email address and to fully set up your account.

3 You can now select friends, businesses or celebrities that you want to follow, or start sending your own Tweets.

Beware

Be careful how much information you divulge in your profile and in your messages, since you won't always know who is reading these details.

131

Facebook

To join Facebook, you require a minimum amount of information and, since it is free, no credit card is needed.

1 Go to www.facebook.com and provide the personal details requested, then click the Sign Up button

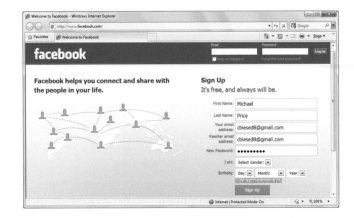

2 Copy the text displayed. This is a security check to prevent automated responders creating accounts

3 Facebook offers to search your address book to identify friends already on Facebook, but you can skip this step

4 You'll be asked to fill in a more complete personal profile, and to submit a photo, but you can skip these steps again

5 Respond to the email message that Facebook sends to you, thus confirming the validity of your email address

6 Sign in to your email account, locate the message from the Facebook Team, and select the hyperlink

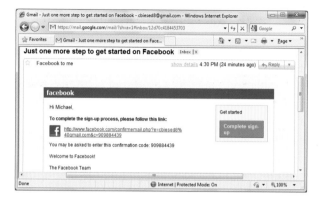

Hot tip

You should take things slowly, until you get used to the system, then you can decide how much information to reveal, and how you will contact your friends and colleagues.

7 When you return to Facebook, you are asked to provide more information about yourself again

8 Before giving more details, scroll down to step 6 to learn about privacy in Facebook

Don't forget

The settings you choose control which people and apps can see your information. You can share your information with friends, friends of friends, or everyone.

RSS Web Feeds and Slices

If you are interested in any regularly changing website, you may be able to keep up to date with the changes without having to actually visit the site. Most such sites now offer RSS feeds or web slices. These avoid logging on to the sites, just in case there are some changes, or subscribing to different newsletters for each site.

Originally supported through special software, support for RSS is now built in to your browser. This lets you know when feeds and slices are available, and helps you view and subscribe to them.

Hot tip

RSS stands for Really Simple Syndication and it is a mechanism for distributing lists of headlines, update notices and additions. A Web Slice allows you to subscribe to a specific portion of a web page.

1 When you visit a website, Internet Explorer automatically searches for RSS feeds and web slices

2 The greyed RSS icon on the browser toolbar indicates that no feeds or web slices have been detected

Beware

Some websites don't use the RSS icon but have a dedicated RSS web page to list the feeds that are available. For an example, see www.reuters.com/tools/rss.

3 When the RSS icon turns orange and (optionally) a sound is played, you know that feeds have been detected

4 A green RSS icon means that web slices (with or without feeds) have been detected on that web page

134

5 Click the arrow next to the RSS icon to list the feeds

6 Select an RSS feed name to view the current news items

7 Click Subscribe to this Feed, then click the Subscribe button to add it to the list of feeds managed by your browser

8 Click the Favorites button then click the Feeds tab to view the feeds being monitored

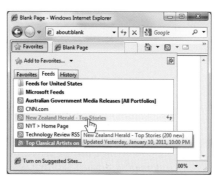

9 Select a feed to view the contents

135

Settings for Feeds

To change settings for your RSS feeds

1 Click Tools, then Internet Options, and then select the Content tab

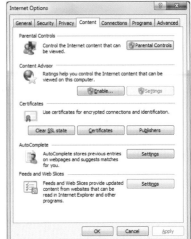

2 Locate the Feeds section and click the Settings button

3 Choose to automatically check feeds for updates and set the frequency

Some feeds provide a link to View Feed Properties link, where you can make adjustments, such as the number of items to be retained.

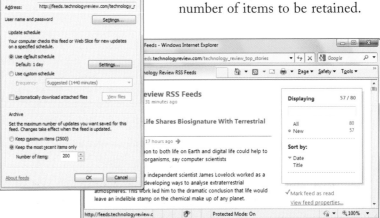

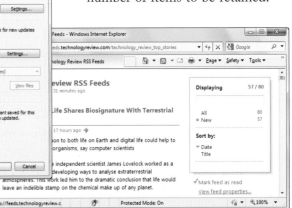

Genealogy on the Internet

The Internet can also be the place to locate personal information. If you are new to Genealogy, there are numerous tutorials online to help you get started. For example:

 1 LearnWebSkills   www.learnwebskills.com/family/

This is a self-paced tutorial designed for beginner genealogists with basic computer and Internet skills.

Other Genealogy websites that may help you locate the tools and information you need include:

2 Cyndi's List   www.cyndislist.com/

Cyndi's List provides a categorized and cross-referenced index to reliable and trustworthy genealogical research websites and resources on the Internet. Click the Topical Index to get started.

Hot tip

There are literally thousands of websites and databases available on the Internet with the records and information you need to help trace your family tree.

Hot tip

You will be researching your own ancestors while learning to use online databases and other genealogical resources.

137

Don't forget

Cyndi's List can act as an excellent starting point for your online research.

...cont'd

3 FamilySearch **www.familysearch.org**

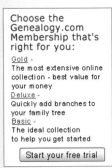

At the FamilySearch website, you can view many records from the extensive family history library maintained by The Church of Jesus Christ of Latter-day Saints

4 Genealogy.com **www.genealogy.com/**

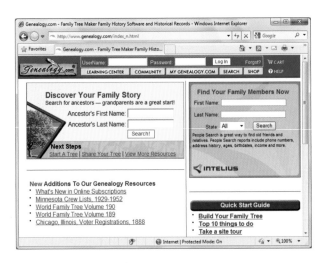

Choose the Genealogy.com Membership that's right for you:

<u>Gold</u> -
The most extensive online collection - best value for your money
<u>Deluxe</u> -
Quickly add branches to your family tree
<u>Basic</u> -
The ideal collection to help you get started

Start your free trial

Genealogy.com provides three levels of service, depending on the range of data collections you want to access. There's also a free trial, so you can make sure that the service is suitable for your needs before you commit yourself completely.

8 Spreadsheets

Spreadsheets are a valuable tool, allowing you to manipulate data and perform calculations with speed and efficiency. They include functions to automatically total or average sets of values, and you can create graphs and charts to explore the information. There are pre-defined spreadsheets to help you handle the most frequently required tasks.

Spreadsheets

A spreadsheet is a computerized version of a ledger sheet, an electronic tool for manipulating numbers. It is designed for listing and calculating quantities and values in a wide range of activities, from budgeting and financial analysis, to forecasting and scientific study. The huge advantage of spreadsheets is that once the data is entered, formulas can be created to perform calculations quickly and easily. When any of the component data is changed, the spreadsheet formulas automatically recalculate to reflect the amendment.

Visicalc was the first electronic spreadsheet, followed soon after by Lotus 1-2-3. Microsoft introduced Excel, which became its main product for Windows. It provides a wide range of functions, including database and query management, pivot tables and what-if scenarios and a full graphing facility.

1 Open Excel to view a standard blank spreadsheet or worksheet. Three worksheets are provided, but more can be added. One or more worksheet comprises a workbook

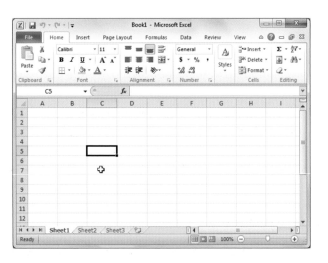

2 Data is entered into cells in columns and rows. Column labels are letters A-XFD, rows are numbered 1-1,048,576

3 A cell is the intersection of a column and row and has a cell or grid reference. The current cell reference, C5, is displayed in the Name Box

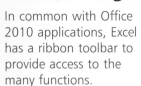

Input Data

1 Both text and numeric data can be entered into a cell. Type your first entry (the worksheet title) and press Enter. The text is stored in the cell and the cursor automatically moves down to the next cell

2 Continue entering your column of data. The text is automatically aligned to the left of the cell

Hot tip

Numbers are aligned to the right of the cell automatically. Initially, trailing zeros are dropped, 2.25 would display as 2.25 but 5.50 would display as 5.5 for example. See page 144 on formatting numbers.

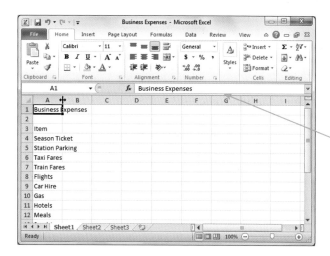

Don't forget

The Name Box and the Formula Bar indicate the current cell and its contents (A1). B1 is empty, although it looks as though it contains some text. If you typed in cell B1, the text in A1 would appear truncated.

3 To widen column A to accommodate the length of the text, position the cursor on the header between the A and B to get the double headed arrow. Then drag to fit, or double-click to widen the column to the longest entry

Navigation

- Home key takes you to column A

- End key + directional arrow goes to the end of the current data range in the direction pressed

- Ctrl+Home goes to A1

- Page up and Page down moves a full screen at a time

- Type a name in the Name Box to go to a named range

- Press the F5 function key and type a cell address to Go To

Fill and Copy

To enable swift data entry, Excel provides the Fill tool. It can be used to fill columns or rows with standard entries, such as days of the week or months. It can also be used to replicate standard data, such as regular amounts. For example:

1 Type Sep in cell B3 and then position the cursor on the bottom right hand corner of the cell. When it changes to a large plus

sign, drag across row 3 to fill with the following months of the year

	A	B	C	D	E
1	Business Expenses				
2					
3	Item	Sep			
4	Season Ticket			Nov	
5	Station Parking				
6	Taxi Fares				

2 Expense items, such as season ticket and parking, are likely to be a regular sum each month. Complete the entries for

	A	B	C	D	E
3	Item	Sep	Oct	Nov	Dec
4	Season Ticket	65			
5	Station Parking	17.5			
6	Taxi Fares				
7	Train Fares				
8	Flights				

September and then highlight both cells and use the Fill tool to add the figures for the rest of the months

The Fill tool also works with number patterns, as in the examples illustrated here.

Copy

1 Highlight a cell or range of cells and click Copy on the Home tab. Position the cursor where you wish to place the first cell and select Paste

2 The range that was copied will display a flashing outline. Press the Esc key to remove it

Insert, Delete and Move

With your data entered into the spreadsheet, you may find you have omitted a category or misaligned your figures. To insert a column or row:

1 Click on the row header and select Insert, Insert Sheet Rows. The row will be inserted above the selected row

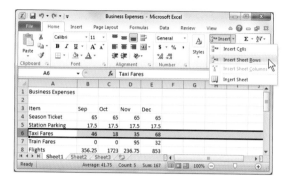

2 For columns, the procedure is the same. With columns selected, the program defaults to Insert columns. The new column will be inserted to the left of that selected

3 To delete the contents of the selected cell or range, just press the Del key. To remove a row (or column) completely, select it in the header row and click Delete, Delete Sheet Rows (or Columns)

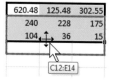

The contents of a cell or range of cells can be moved by selecting them and using Cut and Paste. However, you can also drag them to the new position:

4 With the range highlighted, move the mouse pointer to the edge of the cell, where you see a four-headed arrow

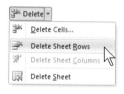

5 Press the left mouse button to drag. Target cells will be indicated and any contents will be overwritten

143

Hot tip

The number of columns or rows you highlight is the number that will be inserted into the worksheet.

Beware

Remember that when you insert or delete a column or row, it affects the whole worksheet and may impact items that are not currently displayed.

Don't forget

You can change the contents of a cell by typing new data. Press F2 to edit the contents of a cell without completely retyping it. Don't use the spacebar to delete the contents of a cell. This puts a space into the cell that is subsequently treated as text, not as a blank, and this may cause problems.

Format the Data

Numeric data can be presented in a spreadsheet as percentages, dates or scientific notation. In a new spreadsheet, the General, i.e. generic format, is used, meaning that text and numbers are displayed as entered. Numbers are aligned to the right of each cell and trailing decimal zeros are dropped. To change the number of decimal places displayed:

1 Select the range of cells to format and on the Home tab, click the Increase or Decrease decimals button

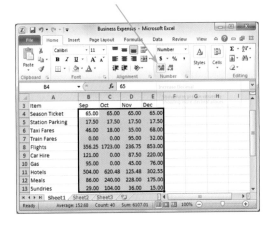

2 Alternatively, for the example illustrated, click the down arrow on General and choose Accounting or Currency

3 Use the Alignment button to align text to the right of the selected cells to match the numeric data and the Fill color to highlight headings

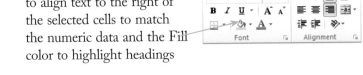

	Nov	Dec
	$65.00	$65.00
	$17.50	$17.50
	$35.00	$68.00
	$95.00	$32.00
	######	######
	$87.50	######
	$45.00	$76.00

4 Excel enables working with dates by allocating all dates a number, starting at 01/01/1900. Data entered as 1/12/09 or 1-12-09 will automatically be formatted as a date

Number	1	40190
Formatted as date	1/1/1900	1/12/2010

Autosum

To total a column or row of figures quickly and easily, Excel provides the Autosum function.

Σ AutoSum ▾

1 Position the cursor in the next adjacent cell below the column of figures, then click the Autosum button on the Home tab in the Edit section

2 The formula is entered for you, with the outlined cells suggested as the range to be totalled

SUM	▾	× ✓ *fx*	=SUM(B4:B13)	
	A	B	C	D	E
3	Item	Sep	Oct	Nov	Dec
4	Season Ticket	65.00	65.00	65.00	65.00
5	Station Parking	17.50	17.50	17.50	17.50
6	Taxi Fares	46.00	18.00	35.00	68.00
7	Train Fares	0.00	0.00	95.00	32.00
8	Flights	356.25	1723.00	236.75	853.00
9	Car Hire	121.00	0.00	87.50	220.00
10	Gas	95.00	0.00	45.00	76.00
11	Hotels	504.00	620.48	125.48	302.55
12	Meals	86.00	240.00	228.00	175.00
13	Sundries	29.00	104.00	36.00	15.00
14	Total	=SUM(B4:B13)			
15		SUM(**number1**, [number2], ...)			

Sheet1 / Sheet2 / Sheet3

3 Click the tick on the Formula bar or press Enter to accept the range

4 The outlined range is merely a logical suggestion. Use the mouse to select an alternative range. In this example, two rows are totalled in one calculation - B4:E5

	A	B	C	D	E	F	G	H
3	Item	Sep	Oct	Nov	Dec			
4	Season Ticket	65.00	65.00	65.00	65.00			
5	Station Parking	17.50	17.50	17.50	17.50	=SUM(B4:E5)		
6	Taxi Fares	46.00	18.00	35.00	68.00	SUM(**number1**, [number2], ...)		
7	Train Fares	0.00	0.00	95.00	32.00			

Readily accessible on the Autosum button are other frequently used functions. These work in the same way, for example:

Σ AutoSum ▾
- **Σ** Sum
- Average
- Count Numbers
- Max
- Min
- More Functions...

1 Position the cursor at the end of the data and click Autosum, Max to discover your maximum outlay

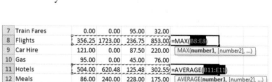

7	Train Fares	0.00	0.00	95.00	32.00	
8	Flights	356.25	1723.00	236.75	853.00	=MAX(B8:E8)
9	Car Hire	121.00	0.00	87.50	220.00	MAX(**number1**, [number2], ...)
10	Gas	95.00	0.00	45.00	76.00	
11	Hotels	504.00	620.48	125.48	302.55	=AVERAGE(B11:E11)
12	Meals	86.00	240.00	228.00	175.00	AVERAGE(**number1**, [number2], ...)
13	Sundries	29.00	104.00	36.00	15.00	
14	Total	1319.75	2787.98	971.23	1824.05	

2 Select Autosum, Average for your average spend

Beware

When totaling rows, always check the range Autosum suggests. With figures in cells above it, Autosum will revert to adding columns.

Don't forget

Use the same procedure to calculate spreadsheet rows.

Hot tip

With one column or row totaled, use the Fill tool to copy the formula to the rest of the worksheet.

Beware

Avoid gaps in your data, as the outline around the data will stop at a blank row or column.

Calculation

As seen on the previous page, the Autosum function allows you to total columns and rows of data with ease, but there are times when a simple formula is required, and you have to create it yourself.

1 Click in the cell where you wish to place the calculation and type an equals sign (=). This is a signal to the spreadsheet that this is a formula. Then type, for example, A2*B2 to multiply the contents of those cells together. If the content of either cell changes, the result changes

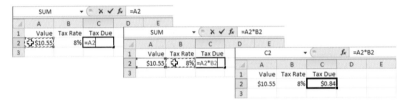

2 Instead of typing, you can use the mouse to select target cells. For example: click in cell C2 and type = then click on A2, type the operator * and click on B2. Then press Enter or click the tick in the Formula bar

3 Cell C2 shows the result of the calculation. The Formula bar shows the contents of the cell, i.e. the actual formula

Absolute cell references

Formulas use cell references that are based on the relative position of the cells to the formulas. This means that you can copy formulas from one column or row to the next. To copy a formula based on one particular cell, as in the example shown, you need to use an absolute reference. An absolute reference includes the $ sign to fix either the column, the row or both. For example:

$D2 for absolute column
D$2 for absolute row
D2 for absolute cell

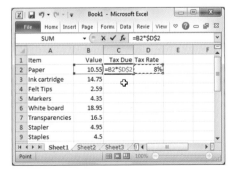

Functions

As well as the very useful Autosum, Excel provides a library of functions to enable a wide range of calculations. To view the list of functions:

1 Click the Formulas tab on the toolbar. The functions are arranged in categories

2 Select, for example, Logical and then If. The function arguments window opens with the function syntax split into steps

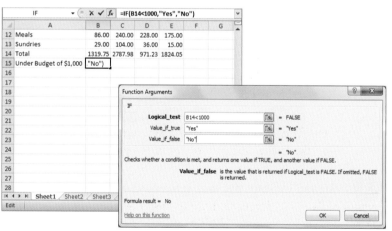

3 Complete the Logical test field by clicking on B14 then typing <1000

4 Add the Value if True (Yes) and the Value if false (No). Then click OK to see the function in the Formula bar

5 To complete the worksheet, use the Fill tool to copy the function across the rest of the columns

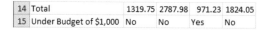

| 14 | Total | 1319.75 | 2787.98 | 971.23 | 1824.05 |
| 15 | Under Budget of $1,000 | No | No | Yes | No |

Hot tip

Click the Insert Function button to see the full list of almost 100 Functions.

Hot tip

If you are unsure of which function you should use, type a description of what you want to do in the Insert Function window.

Don't forget

This example function is intended to discover if our Business Expenses come in under the limit of $1,000.

Auditing Tools

Excel provides auditing tools for you to check the validity of your formulas.

1 Click the Formulas tab to view the auditing options

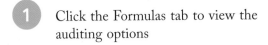

Dec	Jan	Total
65.00	65.00	260.00
17.50	17.50	70.00
68.00	◈	167.00
32.00		Formula Omits Adjacent Cells
853.00		Update Formula to Include Cells
220.00		
76.00		Help on this error
302.55		Ignore Error
175.00		Edit in Formula Bar
15.00		Error Checking Options...
1824.05		

2 Position the cursor on a cell that contains a formula and select Trace Precedents. Select another formula and choose Trace Dependents

	A	B	C	D	E	F
3	Item	Sep	Oct	Nov	Dec	Total
4	Season Ticket	65.00	65.00	65.00	65.00	260.00
5	Station Parking	17.50	17.50	17.50	17.50	70.00
6	Taxi Fares	46.00	18.00	35.00	68.00	167.00
7	Train Fares	0.00	0.00	95.00	32.00	127.00
8	Flights	356.25	1723.00	236.75	853.00	3169.00
9	Car Hire	121.00	0.00	87.50	220.00	428.50
10	Gas	95.00	0.00	45.00	76.00	216.00
11	Hotels	504.00	620.48	125.48	302.55	1552.51
12	Meals	86.00	240.00	228.00	175.00	729.00
13	Sundries	29.00	104.00	36.00	15.00	184.00
14	Total	1319.75	2787.98	971.23	1824.05	6903.01
15						
16	Under Budget of $1,000	No	No	Yes	No	

3 Arrows indicate the data referenced in the formulas

4 Select Show Formulas to have the worksheet display the formula's text, instead of the result of the calculation. Click Show Formulas again to revert to the regular view

	A	B	C	D	E	F
3	Item	Sep	Oct	Nov	Dec	Total
4	Season Ticket	65	65	65	65	=SUM(B4:E4)
5	Station Parking	17.5	17.5	17.5	17.5	=SUM(B5:E5)
6	Taxi Fares	46	18	35	68	=SUM(B6:E6)
7	Train Fares	0	0	95	32	=SUM(B7:E7)
8	Flights	356.25	1723	236.75	853	=SUM(B8:E8)
9	Car Hire	121	0	87.5	220	=SUM(B9:E9)
10	Gas	95	0	45	76	=SUM(B10:E10)
11	Hotels	504	620.48	125.48	302.55	=SUM(B11:E11)
12	Meals	86	240	228	175	=SUM(B12:E12)
13	Sundries	29	104	36	15	=SUM(B13:E13)
14	Total	=SUM(B4:B13)	=SUM(C4:C13)	=SUM(D4:D13)	=SUM(E4:E13)	=SUM(F4:F13)
15						
16	Under Budget of	=IF(B14<1000,"Y	=IF(C14<1000,"Y	=IF(D14<1000,"Y	=IF(E14<1000,"Yes","No")	

Manage Your View

When working with worksheets larger than your monitor size, column and row labels disappear from the screen, making it difficult to align data. To keep your data labels in view:

1 Position the cursor below the column headings and to the right of the row headings you wish to keep in view

Don't forget

Repeat Step 2, and the options are changed to offer the choice to unfreeze panes.

2 Click the View tab, and Freeze Panes. Freeze as currently selected, or freeze the top row, or the first column

To hide columns or rows within the worksheet:

1 In the heading bar, select the columns or rows to hide

2 Click Format on the Home tab, and, in the Visibility section, select Hide

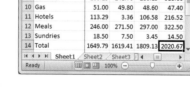

Hot tip

You can also hide columns and rows by selecting them. Right-click the mouse within the highlighted zone and select Hide from the menu.

Don't forget

To unhide, you must highlight a section that includes the hidden area.

Sort Data

The spreadsheet has a number of database facilities, of which Sort is a useful example. To sort a range of data:

1 Position the cursor on the cell you wish to use as the primary sort key, and on the Data tab, click the A-Z to sort ascending, or Z-A for descending. This works with both alphabetic and numeric data

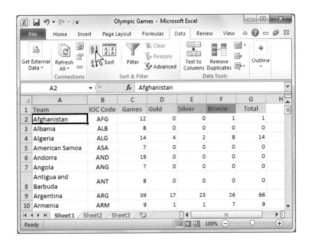

150

2 Select the Sort button for a greater choice of options. Click the arrow to choose a primary field, and a Sort Order

3 Click Add Level to add a second and more sort orders and then click OK when finished

4 Data can also be sorted in date order

Filter Data

The Filter tool, on the Data tab, allows you to select by specific criteria and temporarily screen out unwanted data. For example:

1 With your cursor within the data range, click the Filter button. This adds a series of down arrows to the header line of your data

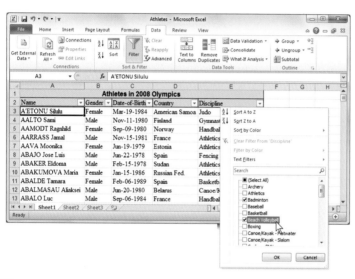

2 Click the arrow on your selected field and choose your criteria, one or more sporting activities for example. Then click OK

3 Choose another criteria, Country for example and repeat the process to extract more specific data

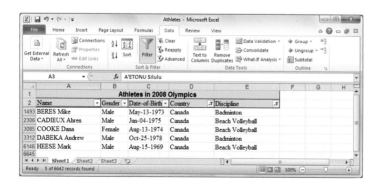

151

Hot tip

Deselect the Select All box to remove all the check marks. Then select one or more categories.

Hot tip

Use the Text Filters on each drop down menu to add qualifiers such as Equals, or Contains.

Hot tip

You can select Clear Filter on an individual column or click Clear on the Data tab to remove all the filters at the same time.

Print the Worksheet

To view the way your spreadsheet will appear when printed:

1 Click the File button, then select Print (or press Ctrl+F2)

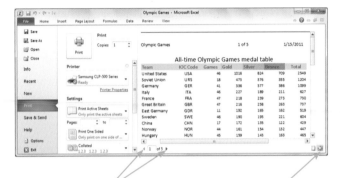

2 Click the Next and Previous Page arrows to view the worksheet

3 Use Page Zoom to see how the worksheet fits on the printed page

4 In the Printer section, choose the printer and adjust its properties

5 In the Settings section, choose to:

Print the active worksheet, the whole workbook or the selected area

Print one-sided or print duplex

Collate multiple copies

Choose portrait or landscape setup

Select the paper size and type

Set the print margins (normal, narrow, wide or custom)

6 When the settings are as required, set the number of copies and click the Print button to start printing

...cont'd

When the worksheet is printed over several pages, you will need to print the column and row labels on every page.

1 On the Page Layout tab, click Print Titles. Click Rows to Repeat at Top and, on the worksheet, select the rows

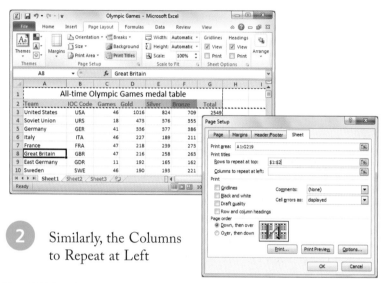

2 Similarly, the Columns to Repeat at Left

To add Headers or Footers to your printed spreadsheet:

1 Click the Header and Footer tab in Page Setup and enter the header or footer text required

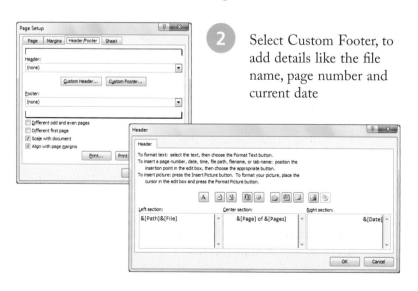

2 Select Custom Footer, to add details like the file name, page number and current date

Don't forget

Select the first row, hold down the Shift key, and select the final row in the heading, to give a range such as $1:$2. Similarly, for columns you'd have $A:$B.

Hot tip

When you print the worksheet with the formulas showing (see page 148), tick the boxes to print Gridlines, and Row and Column headings.

153

Don't forget

File name, date and page number are all examples of autotext. They will be updated automatically the next time you print the worksheet.

Charts

Graphs and charts help to illustrate data and to highlight trends, patterns and fluctuations.

1 Select the range of data that you wish to chart. This should usually include either a column or row heading

2 On the Insert tab, choose the type of chart you prefer and then select from the options available

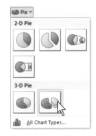

3 The chart will be displayed within the worksheet, with a legend and a chart title

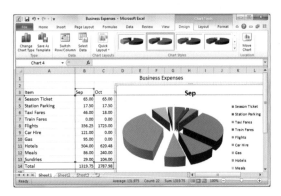

4 Click Quick Layout to view different pie chart designs that include adding values and percentages

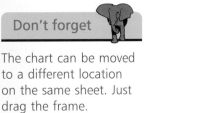

5 Select the Move Chart Location button to put the chart on its own separate sheet

To create a chart with multiple sets of data:

1 Choose rows of data for Sep to Dec, click Insert and then Chart, Column, 2-D Column

2 Select Chart Tools, Design and click the Select Data button

3 Review the data series and revise, if desired, then click OK

4 To add a title, select Chart Tools, Layout, then click Chart Title and choose the position, e.g. Above Chart

5 When the Chart Title

Chart Title

frame is added to the chart, click inside it to add the required title text

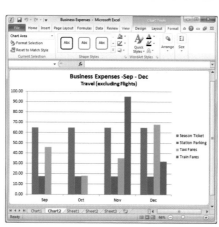

6 Select Chart Tools, Format to make changes to the styles used

Templates

There is a large number of pre-formatted spreadsheets included with Excel and many more are available on the Microsoft website.

1 Click the File button and select New to view the lists

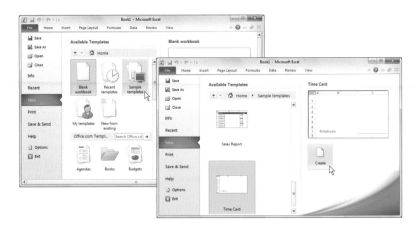

2 Select Sample Templates and choose a template, such as Time Card, then click the Create button

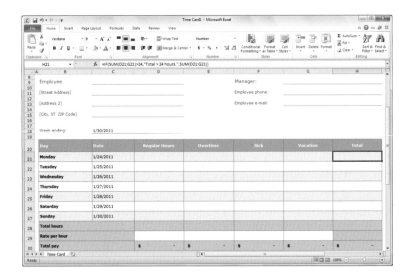

3 A new worksheet called Time Card1 and on that template will be opened, and you can view the design layout, formatting and predefined formulas provided

9 Music and Speech

A soundcard can bring your computer to life, allowing you to play music from audio CDs or digital files, listen to radio broadcasts over the Internet, and play videos with audio tracks. With a microphone, you can even dictate to your computer.

Soundcard and Speakers

The original personal computer included an internal piezoelectric speaker that was capable of only playing one tone at a time. It was really only suitable for warning and error beeps, but with sophisticated programming, it could play music and sound effects. Fortunately, today's computers are equipped with soundcards and speakers that can rival high fidelity audio systems.

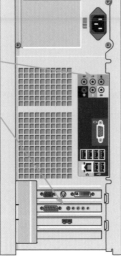

The soundcard will provide connections for various types of speakers ranging from simple stereo speakers to multiple speaker sets with surround sound capability.

158

To check the speaker configuration on your computer:

1 Select Start, Control Panel, then Hardware and Sound, then Manage audio devices, from the Sound section

2 Select Speakers and then click the Configure button, then click Next to complete the specification

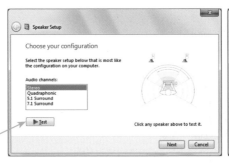

Play Audio CDs

A basic function of your soundcard and speakers is to play an audio CD (assuming, of course, you have a DVD/CD drive).

1   Open the CD or DVD drive, insert an audio CD and then close the drive

2   The AutoPlay panel will be displayed

3   Choose Play audio CD using Windows Media Player

Playing commences but the CD is initially treated as an unknown album and no details other than the track numbers and durations will be displayed.

If you are connected to the Internet, Windows Media Player will locate and download information about the CD, and display the album, track titles and the cover image.

Copy Tracks from CD

You can copy songs from the audio CD. This is called Ripping the CD, and Media Player will make file copies that get added to your library. To specify the type of copy:

1 Right-click the Media Player windows and select More options

2 Click the Rip Music tab

3 Set the Format as one of the Windows Media Audio (WMA) file formats, or select the MP3 format for greater flexibility

4 Select the bit rate – higher bit rates give better quality but use up more disk space

5 Click the Start Rip button to extract and compress the tracks

6 Tracks are added to your Music library – a folder for each artist, and subfolders for their albums

Media Player Library

1 When the CD has been copied, click the Switch to Library button

2 Select Music to display the contents of the Music library, by artist and track

3 Select Artist or Genre to group all the associated albums

4 You can also display the music by individual albums, arranged alphabetically by title

Don't forget

The initial contents of the library are from the Sample Music folder created when Windows was installed. However, you can add tracks from your audio CDs or from Internet downloads.

Hot tip

Click Organize and select Customize navigation pane, to group music by other properties, such as year, rating or composer.

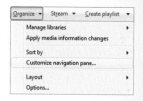

Hot tip

Double-click a group to display the individual tracks it contains, arranged by album.

Download Music

You don't have to own the CD to add tracks to your Media Player library. Download music from an Online Store.

1 Click the arrow on the Online Stores tab and select Browse all Online Stores

Hot tip

The stores offered depend on which country or region you have selected for your system. However, the online store may identify your actual location from your IP address and may restrict services to some regions.

2 Choose a category, then select a store from the list provided, for example: click Music and then Farolatino Music

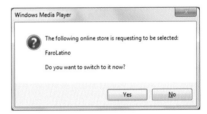

3 Click Yes to confirm that you want to switch to that store

Hot tip

You'll be asked to confirm your registration via your email account.

Confirm Registration Process

4 Provide your name and email plus a user name and password to register

5 You can now login to the music site, with your user name and password

6 Select a category, use Find to locate an artist, album or song, or select one of the highlighted artists to list their albums

163

7 Click the green arrow to review the contents of an album

8 Select View Videos to see the track being performed, listen to the first 30 seconds online, or choose Download

Internet Radio

If you just want to listen to music without saving it on your computer, Media Player can link you to Internet radio stations.

Hot tip

The Media Guide is a website that provides links to media files and Internet content for music, movies, TV, games and web based radio.

1 Click the arrow on the Online Stores tab and select Media Guide

2 Select the Internet Radio option

Don't forget

You can select a list of radio stations to suit a particular music genre or other content, such as news and sport.

3 Search by keyword, scroll the list of stations or select a category, New Age music for example

Hot tip

The Editor's Picks are displayed, but you can click Show All to see the full list for the selected category.

4 Review the Editor's Picks or scroll the whole list to select a station you'd like to try, then click Listen

5 The selected radio station begins to play

6 Select Visit to open the website for the station

7 While the station plays, you can read news items or participate in forums. You can also change channels

8 Close the browser to return to the Media Player

If you want to return to a radio station that you played earlier, select Media Guide and Internet Radio, you'll find a list of recently played stations. Click Listen for the one you want.

1 Click Switch to Now Playing, to display the Player mode

2 To return, click Switch to Library

Windows Media Center

If you have Windows Home Premium, Professional or Ultimate, these have Windows Media Center, which provides another way to manage your multimedia functions and can turn your computer into a complete home entertainment system.

1 Click Start, then All Programs and select Windows Media Center

2 Choose Custom setup to personalize the configuration

3 You can optimize your display, set up your speakers or choose to arrange your media libraries

4 The Media Center includes pictures & videos, music, TV & movies, sports, online media and supporting tasks

5 The Music function gives you full access to your music library and allows you to select albums and tracks to play

6 You can watch shows, movies, trailers and clips via Internet TV and (if you have a TV tuner) set up live TV

7 Media Center provides you with full control of your computer, right through to the System Shutdown process

STARTUP AND WINDOW BEHAVIOR

Always keep Windows Media Center on top

✓ Show a warning before displaying Web pages that are not designed for Windows Media Center

✓ Start Windows Media Center when Windows starts

✓ Show taskbar notifications

Speech Recognition

One way to interact with your computer is to simply tell it what you want, with Windows Speech Recognition. To set this up:

1 Click Start, Control Panel, Ease of Access, then Start Speech Recognition

2 Select the type of microphone that you'll be using, a headset microphone being best for speech recognition

3 Follow the advice to position the microphone effectively

4 Read the text aloud so the microphone volume can be set

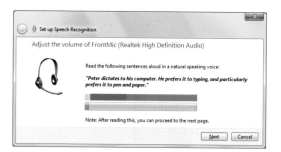

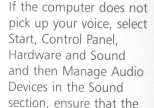
5 Choose Manual activation mode or Voice activation mode

6 Choose to run Speech Recognition when Windows starts

7 Click Start Tutorial to learn about the basic features

Talking to Your Computer

1 Follow the instructions on each page and say or click Next to continue through the sections of the tutorial

2 Select Ease of Access and click Speech Recognition, then choose Train your computer to better understand you

3 Read out loud to let the computer learn how you speak

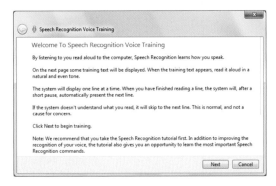

When you start Windows, Speech Recognition will start up and switch itself into Sleeping mode, or turns listening Off (depending on the activation mode you have set).

To see the functions and options offered:

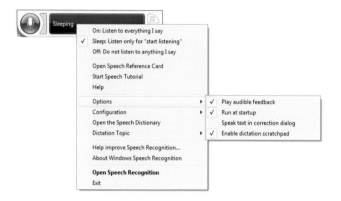

Speech Recognition turns listening off when you have set manual activation mode, but chooses Sleeping for voice activation mode.

Hot tip

It allows you to start and stop applications, say any of the commands or options offered for the active window, or dictate text content, such as documents and email. If in doubt, it offers a suggestion or asks for further information.

171

1 Right-click the Speech Recognition bar

2 Select Sleep, if not already in voice activation mode

3 Say *Start listening* (or click the button on the bar)

4 Say *What can I say?* to view the Speech Reference Card

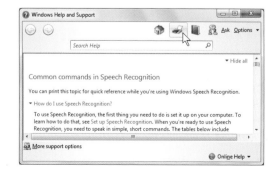

Don't forget

Note how the Speech Bar button changes color as it changes modes.

Text to Speech

You can let the computer talk to you, using the text to speech facilities of the Narrator application.

1. Press the Windows Logo key + U to open the Ease of Access Center and select Narrator (or press Spacebar when Narrator is highlighted)

2. Narrator starts up and you can select the main settings to control what text will be read out

3. Click the Voice Settings button to adjust the voice

There is only one voice currently available, but it does sound very natural. Adjust the speed, volume and pitch to suit your preferences. Narrator will read the contents of the screen, including the text content of programs like Notepad, WordPad, and Windows Help and Support.

4. Click the Help command to see a list of keyboard shortcuts, such as:

   Insert+F8 (read current document)
   Insert+F6 (read current paragraph)
   Insert+F4 (read current word)
   Ctrl (stop Narrator from reading text)

172

10 Photography

Optimize the possibilities of digital photography by using your computer. It can enable you to organize your photos, add effects, create slide shows and make movies. You can display your digital photographs and videos on your TV through your DVD player, print them, or share them with your family and friends on the Internet.

Digital Photography

Digital photography uses electronic technology rather than film to capture images. These images can be displayed, stored, printed, enhanced and shared using software facilities on your computer or at specialized websites on the Internet.

When you take a picture with a digital camera, the image is stored on a memory card within the camera. The storage capacity of the card determines how many pictures you can take before you must download them onto your computer or erase them. Memory is extendable, you can buy an extra card, or a larger capacity card, you can then take more pictures before you need to free up space.

Resolution

The higher capacity also means that you can capture pictures at a higher resolution. Picture resolution is measured in pixels (picture elements). Typically, camera resolution is counted in mega pixels or millions of pixels. Most cameras allow you to set a resolution level, but it's best to take pictures at the highest resolution level, thus getting the clearest image possible. However, the higher the resolution of the picture, the lower the number of images you can store. Also, if you are taking snaps simply for emailing, then choose a lower resolution.

Resolution	Number of pixels
9 million	3456 x 2592
5 million	2560 x 1920
2 million	1600 x 1200
0.3 million	640 x 480

Zoom Factors

When selecting a camera, another consideration is the degree of zoom that the camera can achieve. Cameras have both optical and digital zoom, but the most important is optical. This uses the capabilities of the camera lens to bring the subject closer, enlarging the image before it is stored as pixels.

Digital zoom magnifies the picture by cropping it to select only the specific area after it has saved it as pixels. You can use digital zoom and cropping on your computer using the editing software that comes with the camera, or a program like Windows Photo Gallery. Zooming and cropping on your computer gives you better control over the process.

Hot tip

Memory cards come in many sizes and formats. These include Secure Data (SD), Multimedia Cards (MMC) and Compact Flash (CF). You should check to make sure that you purchase the correct card for your camera. See page 195 for more information on memory cards.

174

Don't forget

The speed at which the camera writes the image data is also important. Children and animals can move at a great speed and are not necessarily willing subjects!

Other Digital Camera Features

● Antishake mechanism. Digital cameras provide an LCD view finder, which necessitates holding the camera away from you when taking a picture. This may cause camera shake and blurring of photos, especially in low light conditions. The antishake feature minimizes or eliminates this problem.

● LCD lightening, which increases the power to the LCD screen in sunny conditions when the subject may be hard to determine

● Wide angle lens. This can change the aspect ratio from 4:3 to 3:2 or 16:9, for example

● Scene mode. This feature creates a series of optimum settings for the camera that takes into account the usual conditions that prevail at, for example, sunset, in snow, for fireworks, etc.

● Video. The more expensive cameras have a limited video function, enabling you to take clips of events

Cameras are packaged with software, a battery pack and charging facility, a USB cable and an AV cable, which lets you connect the camera directly to the television.

The Example Camera

This camera is the Lumix DMC-TZ5 by Panasonic. It has a 28mm wide angle Leica lens with 10x optical zoom. Its maximum resolution is 9.1 mega pixels and it includes features like Digital Red-Eye and Intelligent Exposure. It is also capable of recording high-definition video at 30 frames per second. There is 50MB built in memory, and a memory card slot for SD and SDHC cards up to 16GB.

Don't forget

Some cameras still have a traditional viewfinder, which may be an asset if you are unsteady.

Don't forget

Before purchasing a camera, check to ensure that your computer meets the minimum requirements of the camera and software.

Install the Software

Hot tip

Adobe Reader and Quick Time are free programs and readily available on the Internet. If the version on the PC is newer than the version on the CD, the installation wizard will not overwrite the existing version and the programs will fail to install. This will not affect the operation or functions of the new photo software.

1 Insert the CD supplied with your camera and select to Run the program

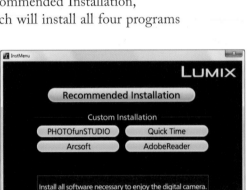

2 Follow the on-screen prompts to allow the program and then select Recommended Installation, which will install all four programs

3 The Setup Install shield will step through the process, covering items like terms and conditions, the destination folder for the files, desktop shortcut, photo acquisition and language

Don't forget

Each of the programs will be installed in turn, with a similar set of prompts.

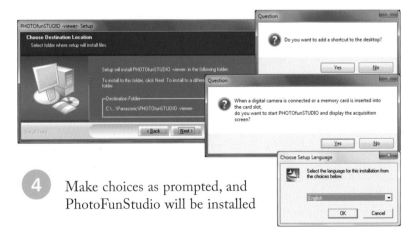

4 Make choices as prompted, and PhotoFunStudio will be installed

Transfer the Photos

1 Ensure that the camera is connected to the mains, or, alternatively, that it has sufficient power to complete the upload to the PC

2 Connect the camera to the computer using the USB cable or cradle provided and turn on the camera

3 The computer should recognize that new hardware is attached and install the drivers for the camera. This will only happen the first time

Installing device driver software
Click here for status.

MATSHITA DMC-TZ5 USB Device
Device driver software installed successfully.

Your device is ready to use
Device driver software installed successfully.

4 The Autoplay window shows that the operating system is treating the camera as removable storage and has allocated it a drive letter.

5 Click the Close button, since the camera software will start up and import the pictures

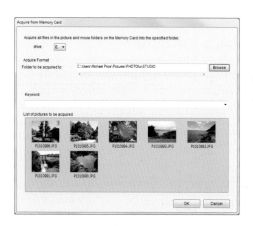

6 The application PhotofunStudio offers a preview of the photos and indicates where they will be stored

Don't forget

You may have been supplied a card reader with your camera, or have a suitable reader in your computer, in which case, you will need to extract the memory card from the camera and insert it in the reader.

177

Hot tip

With PhotofunStudio, you can accept the folder suggested, or browse to a different folder. This program will put all the photos into one single folder. Some programs, Windows Live Photo Gallery, for example, will create a folder for each time photos are acquired, usually taking the current date as the folder name.

...cont'd

7 The process is reasonably automated and straightforward

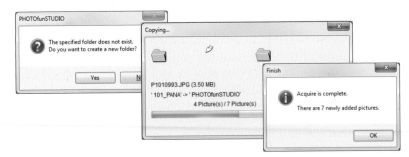

8 When the acquisition is complete, the photos will be displayed, with the Explorer pane showing the folder where the files are stored

9 In common with many other programs that are bundled with cameras, PhotofunStudio has a wide range of tools that will enable you to edit, rotate, add effects and make corrections, such as red-eye or crop to eliminate unwanted items in the photo

10 There are also facilities to create desktop wallpaper, send by email, write to CD/DVD and print

Detach the Camera

When the camera is attached to the computer and switched on, a new icon appears in the Notification area on the bottom right of the desktop. The camera, with its memory card, should be treated like any other removable disk. When you have finished working with it, you should use the Safely Remove Hardware feature.

1 Once the photos have been uploaded to the computer, complete any other action on the memory card, such as deleting pictures

2 Leave the camera switched on but close any windows displaying the camera contents

3 Click the Safely Remove icon in the Notification area and select the correct drive to disconnect

4 When the prompt appears, it is safe to remove the connection, turn the camera off and disconnect the USB cable

Hot tip

This procedure is recommended by the camera manufacturer and constitutes best practice. See page 199 for more information on the Safely Remove Hardware option and the problems with incorrect hardware removal.

179

Upload additional photos

With new photos added to those already on the memory card:

1 Connect the camera as before. This time the software will recognize and acquire only the new images from the card

2 In this instance, the files are appended to the same folder, with other software they may be allocated a new folder

Import Using Windows

Hot tip

You can also access the memory cards or camera storage as normal disk drives (see page 195) and copy files to your hard disk.

If you prefer not to use the software supplied with the camera, you can use features built into Windows.

1 Attach the camera or memory card and select Import pictures and videos using Windows

2 Specify a descriptive tag to be used for folder and file names

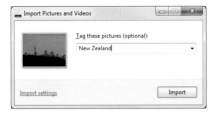

3 Click Import Settings to view or change the target locations for pictures and videos

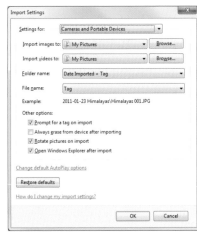

4 Note how the tag is used, and review the other options

Don't forget

Photographs that were imported with the camera software, rather than Windows (or Photo Live Gallery), will not be designated as Imported, and you must select the Pictures folder for them to be displayed.

5 Click OK and Import, the imported pictures and videos are displayed in Windows Explorer

Windows Live Photo Gallery

If you have Windows Live Essentials (see page 27) installed on your system, you can use Windows Live Photo Gallery:

1   When the Autoplay options displays, select Import pictures and videos using Windows Live Photo Gallery

2   Specify a folder name for the new pictures

3   If desired, you can Add tags

Hot tip

If the pictures cover a variety of topics, you can choose to review, organize and group them prior to importing.

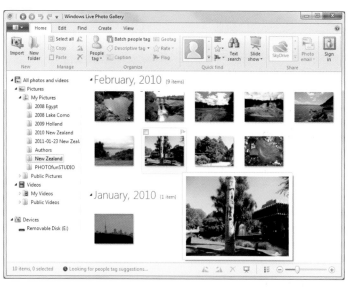

Don't forget

Photographs are date stamped by the camera. They can be selected by date in Live Photo Gallery, so make sure you keep the correct date in the camera.

181

4   Photo Gallery recognizes folders where images are stored and includes them in the navigation pane

5   Select the application icon and click Include Folder to Add folders to the Picture library

Hot tip

You can Add folders to the library from a fixed drive on your computer or on any computer on your local network.

6   To view all the pictures in the library in date order, click Pictures (or click My Pictures to exclude public folders)

Edit Your Photos

Lighten or Adjust Contrast

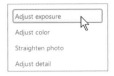

1 Double-click the image in Live Photo Gallery and select the Edit tab

2 Select Fine Tune, click Adjust Exposure and slide the pointers either way until a satisfactory result is achieved

3 You can try out effects and click Revert to Original to undo changes. Select Close File to save the latest changes

4 You can still retrieve the original picture, by choosing Edit and selecting Revert to Original

Adjust Red-Eye

Red-eye can still be a problem in certain conditions, even though cameras now have the built-in double flash to try to eliminate it.

1 Select Edit, Red Eye and draw around the problem area to recolor that part of the image

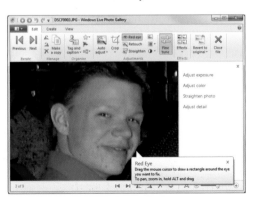

Crop the Image

1 To remove unwanted elements, click Edit and Crop. Use the four-headed arrow to move the frame as required

2 If the frame size should need adjusting, choose from the pre-defined aspect ratios. Then click Apply Crop

Add Captions

1 Select Home, Caption, to add a title to the photo

The title is viewable in Live Photo Gallery, and in Picture Library

Don't forget

Cropping the image is done using digital zoom to magnify an area.

Don't forget

The aspect ratio you should choose for your photo depends on how you wish to view it.

If printing, choose 4 x 6, TV or PC choose 4 x 3, widescreen or HD TV use 16 x 9.

Hot tip

To add visible text, such as greetings or place name, as part of photo itself, you need a more sophisticated editor like Adobe Photoshop.

Print Your Photos

The most cost effective way to view your photographs is to write them to a CD or DVD and view them, either on your computer, on a TV or on a DVD player. (See page 192). There are times, however, when you will want to have them printed. There are four main approaches:

- A dedicated photo printer. These usually print 4 x 6, but some are available to print 5 x 7 or a variety of sizes. You may have to buy the photo paper from the printer manufacturer. Most of these printers can be used with the memory card from the camera, or directly from the camera with Pictbridge software

- Take the memory card or a CD of the photographs to a local printing service. Many are now semi-automated, with the customer running the process

- Upload the photographs to an online photography site, where you can invite friends and family to view the pictures, and have them printed. This is generally the cheapest method

- Print them using your regular color printer. This is best suited to when you want the convenience of an instant print, or if you wish to print a non-standard size

Photo Printing in Windows 7

1 Open Live Photo Gallery and select the pictures to print

2 Click the Application icon, select the Print category and click Print

Hot tip

Using a dedicated photo printer is considered to be a more expensive method. Critics complain about using large quantities of ink and of manufacturers' paper being expensive.

184

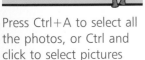

Don't forget

Press Ctrl+A to select all the photos, or Ctrl and click to select pictures individually.

Hot tip

You can access the same Print function in the Pictures Library folder. The only difference is that Live Photo Gallery has the option to Order prints over the Internet.

3 The default is to print one picture per page. Scroll down to view the variety of layouts offered

Don't forget

Note that with four to a page, the print size is 3.5 ins x 5 ins, not the standard 4 ins x 6 ins as in commercial printing.

4 With four pictures to print, selecting a different layout will change the number of pages needed

5 Choose a print quality. Remember that higher quality will slow the printer, since it has to interpolate extra pixels

Hot tip

The options offered will vary depending on the printer you choose. For example, the Lexmark printers offer quality in terms of draft, normal or best. They can also sense the type of paper inserted.

6 Paper quality has the greatest impact on the resulting print. However, remember that some printers cannot handle high gloss finishes. Click Print when ready

Order Prints

If you choose the option to order prints, Windows will access the Internet to locate suitable online photography dealers for your location.

The companies that you investigate will be added to the Print menu, for ease of access in the future.

See page 192 for an alternative way to share photos.

Hot tip

When you click Send Pictures, you will be warned that personal details might be sent to the chosen printing site. You will be able to get an idea of cost, etc. before you register and provide credit card information.

Integrated Facilities

Slide Show

1 With the folder open in Live Photo Gallery, click Slide Show on the Ribbon or the Status bar (or press F12)

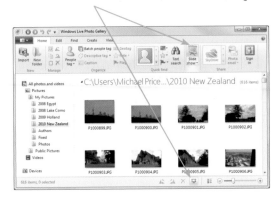

2 The slides will display full screen, with a time delay of approximately five seconds. Advance or redisplay slides with the arrow keys. Press the Esc key to end the show

Email

Take advantage of the link provided to access Windows Mail and easily adjust image sizes as they are attached.

1 With one or more images selected, click Photo email then Send photos as attachments

2 Pick the photo size, using the smaller options if the users have dial-up systems

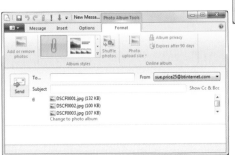

3 Enter the email address and your message in the usual way, then click Send

Video Clips

Video clips have a different file format from a standard photo, and there are several formats used, including .avi, .mov, .mpeg and .wmv. To play a video clip from your camera, you will need a player that supports the specific file format. The Panasonic camera produces a video clip in the .mov format, which is supported by Windows Live Photo Gallery.

To set this program as the default viewer for videos:

1 Click the application icon, select Options, choose the Import tab and click the link Change default autoplay options

 Options

Hot tip

Windows Live Photo Gallery imports other video formats, including .avi, .mpg and .wmv. However, it cannot edit videos. For this, you need Windows Live Movie Maker (see page 188).

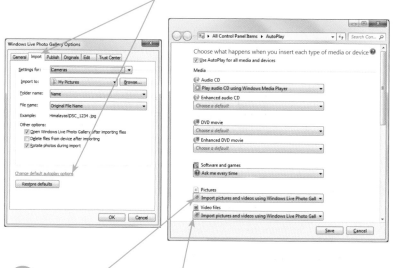

2 For Pictures and Video files, choose to Import using Windows Live Photo Gallery. Then click Save

3 Attach the camera or memory card to import the video clips, which are displayed as single frames with a film-style border

4 Double-click the clip to run the video

Don't forget

A 75 second video clip created a 101 MB file. Video clips can require a considerable amount of storage, even though they use a lower resolution than standard photographs.

Windows Live Movie Maker

Windows Live Movie Maker can be used to give a professional appearance to your photos, videos and video clips by adding transitions and effects, music and voice-over, titles and credits. When finished, you can save the movie to DVD and play it on TV, email it or share it on the web.

You can start with your imported collections of photos and videos:

1 Open Windows Live Photo Gallery, select the folder and choose the items you want to include in your movie

2 Select the Create tab and click the Movie button

3 A new project called My Movie is generated, in the form of a straightforward slideshow. Move the mouse over any slide to view the settings

DSCF0044.JPG
Duration: 00:07.00
Transition: None
Pan and zoom: None
Effects: None

Add Music to Your Movie

1 Click the Add music button, in the Add group on the Home tab

Hot tip

Select enough tracks to match or exceed the duration of your movie.

2 Locate a folder with suitable tracks and select the one you want to add, then click the Open button

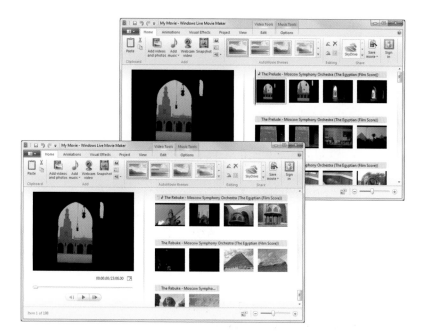

Don't forget

The tracks are assigned in sequence, and change over mid-slide, according to the durations. The music stops when the last slide has been displayed, even if part of the track remains unplayed.

3 Scroll down the photos to see how the tracks are assigned

Play the Movie

1 Click Start on the control bar to display the movie with the music

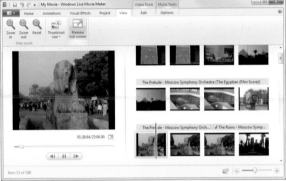

2 Select View, Preview Full Screen to see just the movie

3 Click Back to MovieMaker (or press Esc) to return to the reduced size view with the slides and progress bar

4 Click the Pause button in either view to stop the movie at that point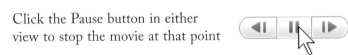

5 Move the mouse pointer over any AutoMovie theme to see the effects, and click to apply

6 Pan and Zoom, for example, adds Title and credit slides, cross fade between slides and automatic pan and zoom

There are numerous options to help you customize the theme:

1 Select Text Tools to edit the textual content of slides

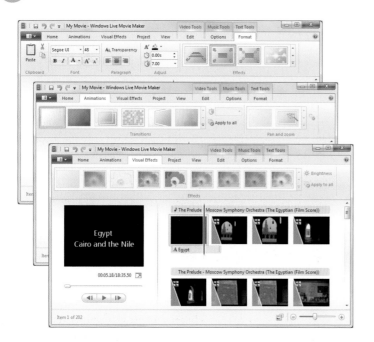

2 Animations offers Transitions, Pan and zoom effects

3 Visual Effects can be applied to selected slides or all slides

Don't forget

In full screen mode, you can click Change Theme and select an AutoMovie theme from the list.

Don't forget

Windows Live Movie Maker also provides a set of Music Tools and a set of Video Tools.

191

Save and Publish Your Movie

My Movie.wlmp
Windows Live Movie Maker Project
98.4 KB

My Movie.wmv
00:23:06
119 MB

1 Click the application icon to display options to save and publish your movie

2 Click Save Project to record the actions taken to define and customize your movie (the photos and music files remain in their original locations)

3 Select Save Movie and choose the purpose, to create a file of the appropriate type containing the completed movie, with copies of all picture and audio files incorporated

4 Creating the movie file and writing it to the drive may take quite a time

This option also allows you burn the movie to DVD or to prepare a lower resolution version to send as an email

5 Select Publish Movie to prepare the movie for publishing on the Internet

6 You can save the movie on your Windows Live SkyDrive or select a service, e.g. Facebook, YouTube

7 You can select Add a Plug-in to find other web services that may be made available for publishing movies online

8 Select Exit to close Windows Live Movie Maker

11 Gadgets and Gizmos

Computer electronics on a smaller scale are applied to create storage devices for many purposes, ranging from digital photographs, videos, maps, driving instructions, or just simple extensions of the storage on your computer. Software functions within Windows or specially installed software for specific devices enhance the function of these devices.

Extra Storage

To see how much disk storage you have on your computer:

1 Select Start and click Computer (or press WinKey+E)

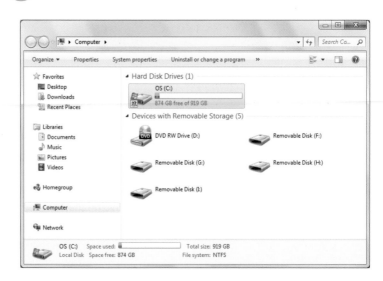

If there's less than 10% disk space available, the capacity bar is colored red rather than the usual blue. You can use Disk Cleanup to free up disk space (see page 222).

2 Look particularly for Removable disk entries which could indicate that you have a media card reader installed

If your computer has a media card reader installed, you'll be able to extend your storage space using memory cards. These come in a variety of shapes and sizes, and may be able to provide as much as 64GB of additional file space, depending on the type and capacity.

Hot tip

The example PC has a 19-in-1 media card reader with four slots that support xD-Picture Card, Smart Media, Compact Flash, Micro Drive, Secure Digital, Multi Media Card and Memory Stick cards.

Each GB of storage on the memory card can store around 300 music tracks, about 350 high definition photos (depending on resolution), or about 30 minutes of video clips. They could also be used as removable disk drives, and used to store data files of various types, documents or spreadsheets for example.

Reading a Memory Card

1 Insert a Smart Media memory card for example

2 Choose the option to Open folder to view files

3 The contents of the memory card will be displayed

4 Select the particular folder

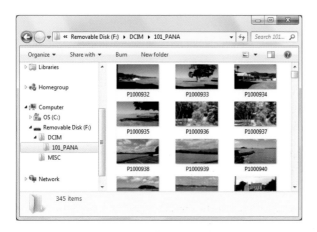

Hot tip

The exact contents of the panel displayed when you insert a memory card depends on the type of files contained. This shows the response when there are picture files on the card.

Don't forget

This is an alternative way to access and copy the photos on your digital camera's memory cards, rather than the supplied software (see page 176).

5 To remove the memory card, click Computer to display the Drive view, select the relevant drive (in this case, G:)

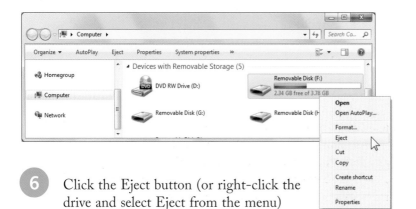

Hot tip

With a multiple drive media card reader, you do not use the Safely Remove option (see page 199) as this would disconnect the whole reader until the next restart.

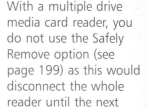

6 Click the Eject button (or right-click the drive and select Eject from the menu)

Flash Drive

Although called a drive, this isn't a mechanical device. It just appears as a disk drive to the computer operating system, and gets accessed in the same way.

Memory cards are fairly delicate. For storage that you can carry around with you, try the more robust USB flash drives that offer anywhere from 1GB to 64GB, in a compact, durable and high speed format. Most USB flash drives have a removable cover over the USB connector. However, some are designed with a sliding mechanism, so the connector is hidden until needed.

In this case, Windows detects that there are audio files on the flash drive, and offers appropriate actions.

196

1 Insert the flash drive into one of your USB ports

2 Windows assigns the next available drive letter and displays the AutoPlay list

3 Select the option required, e.g. Open folder to view files

If there are any programs using the flash drive when you choose Safely Remove and Eject Device, you will be warned.

4 Click the Safely Remove Hardware icon, select the drive, and remove the device when prompted

Netbook USB Drive

Verbatim's Netbook USB Drive provides additional semipermanent storage capacity to a netbook computer ,without increasing its footprint. Though tiny in size, this drive comes with 8 GB, 16 GB or 32GB.

Hot tip

You can see how small the drive is when you compare it to a coin, in this case a Euro (slightly smaller than a Quarter).

1 Insert the flash drive into one of your USB ports

2 Windows installs the device driver software, assigns the next available drive letter and displays the AutoPlay list

3 Select the option required, e.g. Speed up my system, using Windows ReadyBoost

4 You can dedicate the device to ReadyBoost, or allocate just part of the space, leaving the rest for file storage

5 The USB drive will be listed in the Computer folder as a removable drive

◢ Devices with Removable Storage (1)

VERBATIM (E:)
3.38 GB free of 7.38 GB

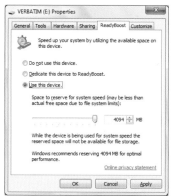

Beware

With the drive assigned to ReadyBoost, you will not be able to remove it without shutting down the system, unless you amend the ReadyBoost Properties to Do not use this device.

6 You can leave the drive inserted in the USB port

External Disk Drive

For larger volumes of data, you can add an external disk drive. This device includes a drive similar to the internal hard disk in your computer, but fitted into a separate disk enclosure. Some such devices use the standard 3.5 ins disk format found in desktop computers. Others use the 2.5 ins drive found in laptop machines, to reduce the power requirements and to avoid the need for a separate power supply unit.

1 Plug in the power adapter, if required, then connect the drive to one of the USB ports

2 If required, Windows installs the device driver software

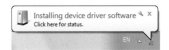 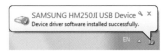

3 Windows assigns a drive letter and runs AutoPlay

4 Select the option required, e.g. Open folder to view files

5 It is listed as a hard disk drive, even though it is removable

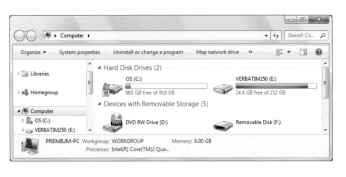

Device Removal

You need to take care when removing drives because Windows may be in the process of updating the contents. To see the options, view the drive properties:

System properties

1 From the Welcome Center, double-click View Computer Details and select Device Manager

2 Double-click Disk Drives to expand the list (or click the white triangle)

3 Right-click the internal hard drive and select Properties

4 Click the Policies tab

For internal drives, Windows will enable write caching to optimize performance. For extra speed, it provides an option to turn off cache buffer flushing. However, this would require some form of power backup on your computer.

5 From Device Manager, right-click a USB connected drive

6 View the Policies for the removable drive

For USB drives, Quick Removal is the default setting. You can select Better Performance, but this isn't recommended due to the potential risk to your data.

Don't forget

Whatever the setting, you must never remove a drive while Windows is in the process of writing information, or you will corrupt the contents and perhaps make the drive unusable.

Don't forget

Right-click the entry for a USB attached drive, in the Device Manager list.

TomTom Go GPS

Don't forget

Other devices include storage facilities, for example: digital cameras (see page 174), personal digital assistants (PDA) and Smartphones (see page 205), or global positioning systems (GPS), e.g. TomTom Go.

Hot tip

You can install the software from the CD provided with the device, but you'll get the most up to date version if you visit the TomTom website.

Don't forget

For illustration, we use TomTom GO 920 and the Windows version of the Home application.

The TomTom Go GPS is an example of a device that functions on a stand-alone basis but connects to your computer for updates, backup and data transfer. This will require computer applications, in addition to device driver software as used by the flash drives.

The TomTom Go uses the Home Dock to connect to your computer via one of the USB ports. It also requires the Home device management application to be installed on your computer.

1 Go to the website **www.tomtom.com/home**, and scroll to the TomTom Home download links

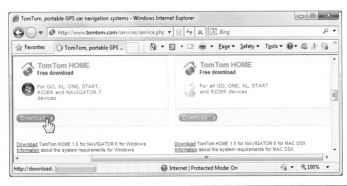

2 Click the link for your type of operating system version and follow the prompts to Save the software to disk

3 When the download completes, click Run to install the software

4 Select the Installer language and the Setup Wizard begins

5 The Wizard will install the Home application

201

6 Install completes and Home will be started up

7 Click Log In to sign on to the TomTom website, using your email address and password

Connect the GPS

Don't forget

While the device is connected to your computer, the battery will be recharged. For a quicker recharge, leave the device switched off.

Hot tip

From Windows, you can store digital pictures and audio tracks on the memory card and play the sound through the GPS speaker (or over the car stereo speakers).

1 Connect the GPS using the Home dock and a USB port

2 Switch on the GPS and press YES to make the connection with the computer

3 The first time you connect, Windows identifies the device and installs the drivers required

4 Choose to work with the Internal Memory or with the Memory Card (if fitted)

5 The Home application will connect to the TomTom server and search for updates for your particular device

6 Select the updates that you want and click Update and Install to apply changes to your device

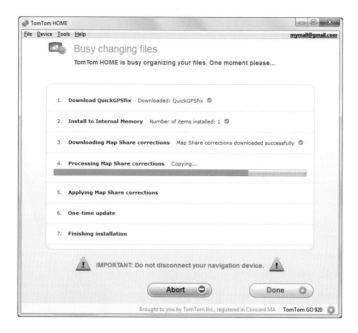

7 When the changes have been applied, click Done to go to the Home menu

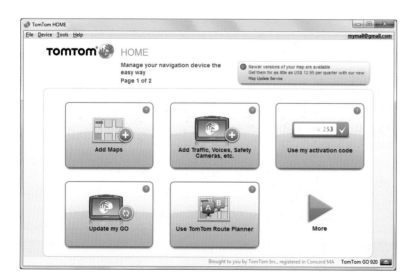

Hot tip

You may be offered a number of updates, but you do not have to apply them all at once. Just click to clear the tick symbol against updates you want to postpone.

Beware

Do not disconnect the device while the update is in progress or you may corrupt the contents. Select Device, Disconnect Device when the changes are complete.

Don't forget

You'll be told when maps are out of date and offered subscriptions to map updates.

Media Players

These connect to your computer so you can transfer the MP3, JPEG, AVI or other media files that they handle.

The device may use computer software such as Windows Media Player or device specific applications, to sync and transfer media files, or the device may simply appear as a removable drive to which you can copy files.

For normal operation, they are stand-alone devices. For storage, they use memory cards (up to 32GB) or hard drives (up to 160GB). They may rely on headphones or external speakers and there may be no display. The Sony Walkman MP3 player, for example, connects to your computer just like a USB flash drive, but stores MP3 or WMA audio files that you can listen to via a set of lightweight headphones.

Media Players handling digital photos usually feature a display, ranging in size from 1.8 ins to 7 ins. They may support multiple types of memory cards, and are often used to complement a digital camera, allowing you to view the photographs more effectively when you are without access to a computer or television. They may also include a built in speaker, useful for replaying audio tracks or video clips with sound.

Windows treats devices like these as removable drives, so you must:

1. Attach the device to your computer and Windows will load the associated software driver and application

2. Amend or supplement the contents of the device, adding appropriate media files from your hard drive

3. Use the Safely Remove Hardware feature when finished with the device, to avoid the risk of losing data

PDAs and Smartphones

The Personal Data Assistant or PDA is a hand-help computer that is fully independent, with its own operating system, Windows Mobile for example. It has its own set of applications, which could include Microsoft Office Mobile, with mobile versions of Outlook, Word, Excel and PowerPoint. Some PDAs go further, adding features like GPS navigation and digital camera capabilities.

When PDA functions are combined with mobile phone capabilities, the devices are known as Smartphones. These are mainly distinguished by their operating systems, which include:

- Blackberry OS, from RIM
- Symbian OS, from Nokia
- Windows Mobile, from Microsoft
- Android, supported by Google
- iPhone OS, from Apple Inc

You'll find that the Qwerty keyboards that were featured on the original smartphones are being replaced by touch screen capabilities, in combination with libraries of applications that can be downloaded onto the smartphone, often for free or for a very small fee. These developments have given iPhone and Android the fastest growth in market share.

To keep up with this trend, Microsoft is replacing Windows Mobile with Windows Phone 7, which incorporates multi-touch capabilities and a new user interface based on a Start screen with Tiles. Mobile phones designed for Windows Phone 7 must meet rigid standards that include a 1 GHz or faster microprocessor, DirectX 9-capable graphics, at least 256 MB of RAM and at least 8 GB of storage. You will also get a 5 megapixel camera with flash, and a multi-touch display with resolution of 800 x 480.

205

Don't forget

The PDA is a stand-alone device with its own storage that can connect to your computer to share functions and data.

Hot tip

The Backberry included a full Qwerty keyboard that was thumb-operated.

Don't forget

You can choose from hundreds of thousands of applications for the iPhone, and even develop your own.

Hot tip

Every Windows Phone must include the same hardware buttons - Back, Start, Search, Camera, volume and On/Off.

Connect Your Smartphone

Don't forget

The built-in camera takes photos up to 2592 x 1944, and videos up to 1280 x 720 at 44fps.

For illustration, we will use the LG Optimus 7 smartphone. This meets and exceeds the Microsoft Windows Phone 7 standards, and features 512 MB RAM, 512 MB ROM and 16GB storage.

To share files between the smartphone and your computer:

1 Connect the smartphone to your PC using the mini USB cable supplied

2 Windows detects and identifies the new device, and downloads the device drivers

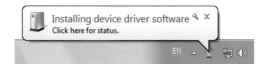

3 The software drivers are installed in turn

Hot tip

The Zune PC application was originally designed for Microsoft's Zune media player. It is now used to manage the synchronization of media files between PC and smartphone.

4 Click Get Software to download Zune to your PC

5 Windows will open the Zune website where you should select Download now to begin the process

Hot tip

You are offered the opportunity to sign up for a free Zune account, but this is not a requirement for synchronizing with your smartphone.

6 Follow the prompts to download the Setup package and accept the license terms

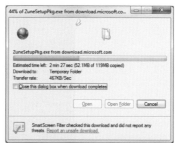

7 Disconnect your smartphone then click the Install button

Don't forget

Note that information about your setup will be sent to Microsoft, unless you clear the box before selecting Install.

8 Setup will prepare your computer and install the Zune software

9 You must allow Windows to restart, to complete the installation

207

Sync Your Smartphone

Don't forget

When you connect your smartphone to your PC with the USB cable, Windows detects the phone and starts the Zune software.

1 The first time you connect your phone, you are prompted to setup the Zune software, and give a name to the phone

Hot tip

You can accept the defaults, initially, and make desired changes later, using the Settings option in Zune.

2 Accept the default settings, or choose to customize Zune

Hot tip

If necessary, you may be prompted to update your phone with the latest features.

3 Provide a suitable name to identify your smartphone (or accept the name suggested, LG LG-E900 in this case)

4 Zune starts up at Quickplay, where you can choose Collections to synchronize media files with the PC

5 Select Music, and choose albums or tracks to drag and drop onto the Phone icon, to copy them to your phone

6 Select Phone, Summary for details of the storage used and still available, and the timing of the latest sync

Home Network

If you have more than one computer, you can share their storage facilities and other devices. To do this, you need to connect them together as a network. This map shows a typical home network:

Wired Computer   Switch   Gateway   Internet

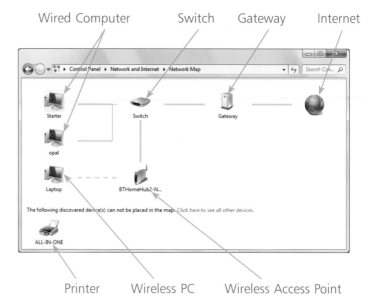

Printer   Wireless PC   Wireless Access Point

The computers are connected via ethernet cables to the network switch, or via a radio link to the wireless access point. A Gateway connects the network to the Internet and this connection can be shared by any of the computers on the network. To add a PC and create or extend a network:

1 If not already fitted, add a network adapter and restart the PC to install the driver

2 The icon in the notification area tells you there is no connection

3 Connect the PC to the network switch with an ethernet cable

4 Windows asks you to specify the location of the network you are joining

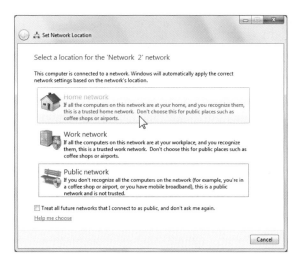

Hot tip

Select Home, for a personal network, or Work for a business network that you share with other users.

5 If the computer is at home on a trusted network, select Home and click View or change Homegroup settings

Beware

Do not specify Home or Work if the network might be accessed by other, unknown users, at a library or Internet cafe for example.

6 Choose which items to share

7 Complete the changes to join the Homegroup

Don't forget

You can share printers and files of selected types with other PCs on the network that are running Windows 7. Windows completes the network definition to add Internet access.

Review Network Settings

Don't forget

You will also find the link to the Network Center on the Connection Status panel (see page 210), which is displayed when you left-click the icon.

1 Right-click the Network icon in the System Tray and select Open Network and Sharing Center

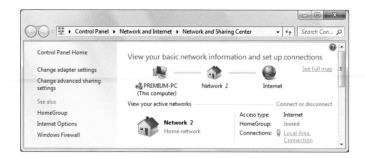

2 This shows the status of your network, Internet and Homegroup connections

3 Click See full map, and Windows creates a network map (see page 210) showing the devices currently connected

4 Select Local Area Connection for details of your network adapter, including the speed and the addresses assigned

5 Scroll down to change your networking settings

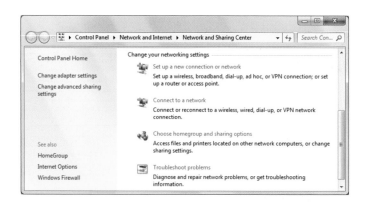

Hot tip

You can also change your adapter network settings, or use advanced sharing settings to give other users additional access to the resources of your computer.

6 Here you set up new connections, connect to networks, change Homegroup settings or troubleshoot problems

Access Network Resources

To see a list of the computers that have joined the Homegroup:

1 Click Start, select the User Name button on the Start menu, and click Homegroup in the navigation pane

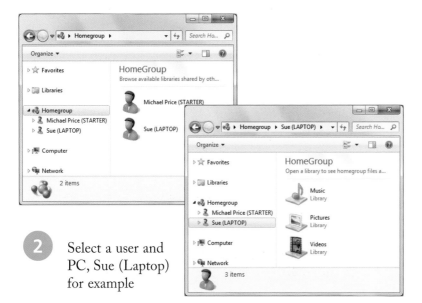

2 Select a user and PC, Sue (Laptop) for example

3 You'll see a list of the libraries being shared by that user on that computer

4 Double-click any library to view or amend its contents

To see all of the computers, including those that are not members of the Homegroup:

5 Open Windows Explorer, as above, and select Network

6 Click a computer name, e.g. Pearl

7 This shows the shared printers and drives

 Hot tip

You'll find Homegroup in any Windows Explorer panel, including Music, Pictures, Documents and Computer.

Beware

Only computers that are currently powered on and active will appear in the Homegroup and Network lists.

213

Don't forget

Network shows all accessible computers, whether connected by ethernet cable or by wireless, whatever their operating systems.

Wireless Network

If your router has wireless capability, you will be able to connect computers in a network with wireless adapters, with no need for network cables.

1 Click the network icon to view the wireless networks available

2 Choose the desired network and click the Connect button

3 Enter the network security code and click OK

214

4 The computer is linked to the network and to the Internet

5 Open the Network and Sharing Center to review settings

12 Manage Your Computer

To keep your computer and Windows operating system working effectively, you need to maintain the system and update the software on a regular basis, using the tools that Windows provides to carry out these tasks.

Windows Update

The Windows 7 operating system needs regular updates to ensure that it remains safe and efficient. To see the level of your copy:

1 Click Start, Control Panel, System and Security, System

2 If it just shows the Windows edition, you have the original release without updates

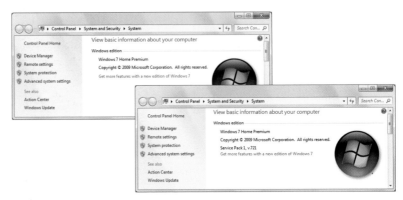

3 Newer releases will be described as Service Pack 1 (SP1) or later. These include many of the updates available

4 To see the status of your system, click Windows Update

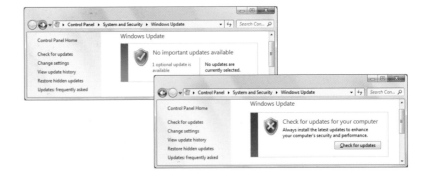

5 If Automatic Updating is not enabled, clicking Check for Updates will let Windows tell you what is available

6 Click Install Updates to download and install the updates

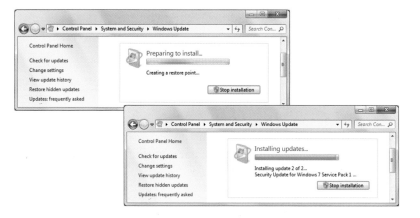

7 Your system may need to restart to complete the updates

Change Settings

1 Open Windows Update and select Change Settings

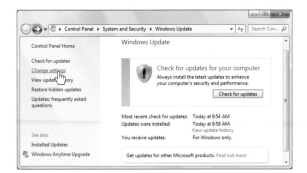

2 Choose how updates are to be installed - automatic
update is recommended

3 You can choose how often and at what time to install the
updates, which are downloaded in the background

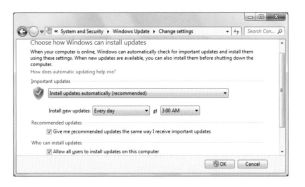

4 Click OK to apply any changes to the settings

Microsoft Update

1 Open Windows Update and select Find Out More about getting updates for other Microsoft products

Hot tip

You can receive updates automatically for other Microsoft products as well as your Windows 7 operating system.

2 Agree to the terms of use, then click the Install button

Don't forget

Microsoft Update will provide updates for Windows, Office, MSN, Windows Defender, and various Windows Server related products.

3 Updates are now detected for the Microsoft products

Hot tip

When you select the Windows Update option, it will now show updates for all the supported products. They'll be applied at the specified time, or you can click Install Updates to get them immediately.

Action Center

The security features in Windows 7 are monitored in the Action Center and you are alerted to problems by messages in the notification area. To open the Action Center:

Move the mouse over the Flag icon in the notification area, an appropriate status message is displayed.

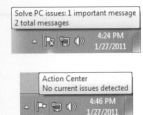

Click the Flag icon to open the Action Center.

1 Click Start, Control Panel, System and Security, Action Center

2 There may be some warning messages (red) or suggestions (yellow)

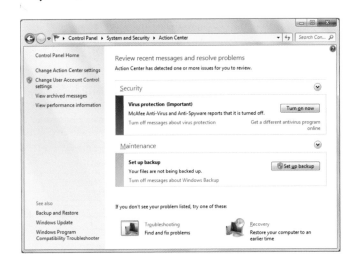

The Action Center offers links to systems management facilities, such as User Account Control, Performance Information and Tools, Backup and Restore and Windows Update.

3 Resolve the issues raised, open Action Center again and the messages will be removed

If you encounter a problem that isn't detected by Action Center, you can try the troubleshooters built into Windows.

1 Open the Action Center and click Troubleshooting

2 Choose the category and an appropriate topic, e.g. Hardware and Sound, for problems with Using a Printer

3 Follow the prompts to identify and resolve problems

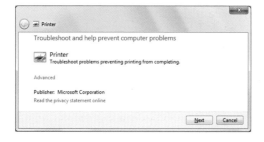

Don't forget

The Action Center has a link to Recovery, part of System Restore (see page 225), to help you remove recent changes that may have caused problems.

Hot tip

If your particular issue isn't listed, click the category to display more troubleshooters, or use the Search box.

Don't forget

Click Advanced to run the troubleshooters as an administrator. This may help to identify more issues to resolve.

221

Maintain Your System

Don't forget

As well as keeping your software up to date, you need to keep your hardware in trim, the harddrive in particular.

1 Open the Computer folder. If the harddisk shows up colored red, you know it's too full

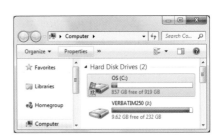

2 Right-click the drive icon and select Properties

3 To free disk space, click the Disk Cleanup button

4 The utility calculates how much space you can free

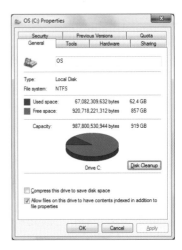

Hot tip

You can choose which categories of file to delete, and view a list of the specific files, if required.

5 Pick which files to delete, click OK, then click Delete Files to confirm

6 The selected files are removed from the disk

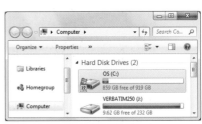

If you are experiencing problems with your hard drive, you can tell Windows to search for and correct errors.

1 Open the Properties for the drive and select the Tools tab

2 Click the Check Now button, then click Start

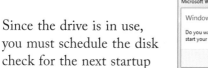

3 Since the drive is in use, you must schedule the disk check for the next startup

4 Before Windows itself starts, the disk check is offered

5 After a short pause, the disk check is applied to the drive

6 Windows will be restarted when the disk check is completed

Don't forget

If you have another disk, not used for the system, select Check Now for this and click Start.

The disk check starts immediately, without shutdown/restart.

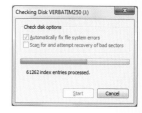

Hot tip

The Windows startup is intercepted and the disk check is offered. Press any key within ten seconds and the check will be bypassed.

Defragment Your Drive

Each time the system makes changes to files on your hard disk, the new data may be stored at a different location. Over a period, the contents of the disk become fragmented. This may slow down the system while it reads from different places to load the parts of the files required. You may be able to improve the performance of your system by defragmenting your hard disk.

Beware

If you select Defragment Disk for immediate action, the process may take minutes or hours, but there's no progress bar, so you'll just have to leave the system until it completes, or select Stop operation to terminate it.

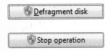

1 From the Tools tab in harddisk properties (see page 223) click Defragment Now

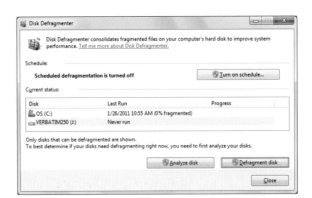

2 Click the button labeled Turn on schedule

Hot tip

If you Defragment on a regular basis, the disk will remain well ordered and the task can be allowed to run in the background.

3 Click in the box to defragment on a scheduled basis. The default is Wednesdays at 1:00 AM (or on the next restart), but you can select Configure Schedule to change the details

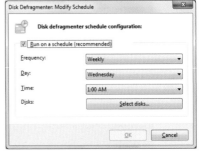

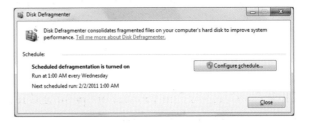

System Restore

By default, Windows creates a restore point every day, and also just before any significant change, such as installing a program or a device or applying a system update.

If things keep going wrong with your system after a change, you can restore it to its previous state and get it working again.

1. Click Start, type part of **system restore** and click that entry when it appears at the top of the Start menu

 System Restore

2. Click Next, then review the recent Restore Points, or click Show more restore points if you need to go further back

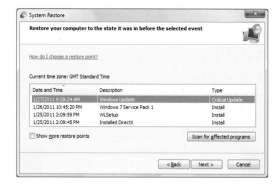

3. When you have found the appropriate restore point, click in the box to accept it, then click Next

4. Click Finish to confirm your restore point and restart the system with the earlier settings

Restart in Safe Mode

1 Click Start, click the arrow next to the Shutdown button and select the Restart option

2 Press F8 repeatedly as the computer restarts (after the initial computer logo but before the Windows logo)

3 The Advanced Boot Options menu will be displayed. Select Safe Mode with or without networking, as you require, and then press the Enter key

There's an alternative way to restart in Safe Mode:

1 Click Start, type **msconfig** and press Enter

2 Click the Boot tab, click Safe boot and choose Minimal, then click OK and click Restart to start up in Safe Mode

3 When you've finished with Safe Mode, run **msconfig**, and choose Normal Startup from the General tab and Restart

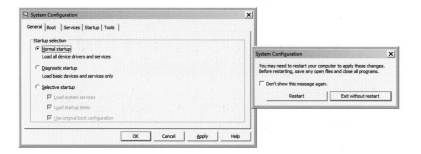

4 To control the startup items, run **msconfig**, click Selective Startup and then the Startup tab

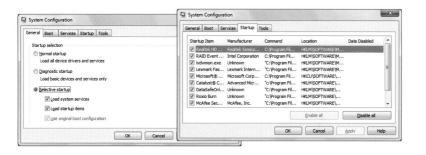

Backup and Restore

To keep your system safe, Windows can help you back up files to a hard disk, to a removable disk or to writable CDs and DVDs. To run the backup process:

1 Select Start, type backup and click Backup and Restore

Don't forget

Alternatively, select Start, All Programs, Maintenance and then Backup and Restore.

2 Select where to save the backup - an external drive is best

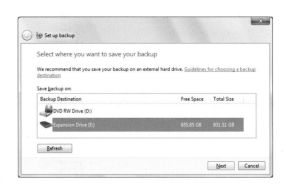

Beware

Backup and Restore to a network drive is only supported in Windows 7 Professional and Ultimate editions.

3 Let Windows choose what to backup (or you can decide), and the files will be backed up on a regular schedule

Hot tip

When you have problems with files, you can use Backup and Restore to recover individual files and folders, or the whole system if necessary.

Adapter Card – a card that plugs into a slot on the motherboard, to add facilities and interfaces for attaching peripheral devices

ADSL – a very fast data transfer method that uses normal phone lines to handle phone calls and data transfer at the same time. Download rates of 512 Kbps up to 8 Mbps

Antivirus Program – a program that finds and eliminates computer viruses

Application – a computer program that provides a particular set of system or business related functions

Backup – a copy of a file or set of files

Bay – place in a computer case to put drives and other devices

BIOS – Basic Input/Output System. A limited set of instructions to the computer which gets it started

Bit – short for "binary digit", a single on/off position in a digital number, and the minimum unit of data

Booting – Starting up the computer and initiating the operating system

Buffer – location for temporary data storage while processing is going on

Button – a graphic which, when clicked, upon executes a command or function

Byte – 8 bits of data, usually a single character

Capacity (Disk) – amount of data that can be stored, measured in megabytes or gigabytes

CD-R – recordable compact disk on which, with the appropriate type of drive, you can copy data files, in a one time write only operation

CD-RW – re-writable CD disk, on which, with the appropriate type of drive, you can save data, erase and write fresh data

Cell – intersection of row and column in a table or on a spreadsheet

Chart – a graphical representation of data

Clip Art – pre-drawn pictures to add to documents

Clipboard – a section of computer memory used to temporarily hold data that has been cut or copied for transfer to another document or location within a document

Columns – columns of data side by side, as in a newspaper

Commands – special codes or keywords that tell the computer to perform a task

Copy – duplicate selection onto Clipboard

Cursor – symbol marking where text will appear when you type

Cut – remove selection from, document and store temporarily on the Clipboard (an area of computer memory)

Data Recovery – a program which tries to recover deleted or damaged data

Data Compression – the method used to store data in less space

Database – a program to manage and manipulate lists, such as addresses, phone lists and inventories

Debug – look for and remove errors in a program

Default – the original settings; what will happen if you don't change anything

Defragment – puts files on a storage disk so that the whole file is in sequence rather than scattered across the disk

Delete – remove selected object (not saved anywhere)

Desktop Publishing (DTP) – a program which gives precise control of where and how text and graphics appear on the page

Directory – a grouping of files, more usually known as a folder

Disk Management – the program involving formatting and defragmenting your disk

Download – transfer a file to your computer from elsewhere on a network or the Internet

DPI – dots per inch. Used to measure printer resolution

Draft Quality – quality good enough for a test print or for internal use

Driver – a file that gives directions to the computer on how to use a device connected to the computer

Edit – make changes in a document

Email – electronic mail - sending messages over a network or internet connection

Executable File – a file that runs a program, also known as an EXE file

External Device – plugs into a port on the computer or connects via wireless communications

Field – a single item that is part of a record in a database

File – something saved on the computer - a document or program

File Transfer – moving a file from one computer to another

File Management – a program to help you create, move, rename, delete files

File Name – has two parts: Filename and Extension, in the form filename.ext

File Type – file name extension that identifies the type of file, doc, txt, htm or exe for example

Folder – a grouping of files

Font – typeface for character set, and associated with Size and Style

Footer – text at the bottom of a page, repeated throughout the document

Footprint – amount of physical desk or floor area that a device requires

Format (Disk) – makes the disk ready for use and removes all existing data

Format (Document) – arranges the appearance of the document by selecting the typeface, font size, spacing of lines and words, etc

Formula – an equation used to calculate values for interest or mortgage payments

Freeware – a program which is given away for free

FTP – File Transfer Protocol. A protocol for moving files between computers

Full Path Name – lists the route to a file starting with the drive name and naming all the folders/directories, like c:\documents\memos\Report4.doc

Gateway – connects networks of different kinds

Graphics – pictures and charts

Hard Copy – Document or file printed on paper

Hard Disk – large capacity data storage device, usually non-removable

Hardware – the physical parts of the computer

Header – area at the top of a page that is repeated on every page of the document

Icon – a small graphic which, when clicked, runs a program, executes a command or opens a document

Input – everything you tell the computer

Input Device – a device used to give the computer data or commands. Includes keyboard, mouse, scanner, etc

Insert – add text at a location without overwriting existing text

Internal Device – plugs into a slot inside a computer

Instant Messaging – a program which notifies you when your contacts are online. You can write them messages which they receive instantly

Justification – alignment of text: left, center, right, full

Keyboard – input device with keys for letters of the alphabet, numbers, and various symbols

Kilobyte – 1024 bytes historically, though often used to represent one thousand (1000) bytes

LAN – Local Area Network. Computers connected together in a single location

Layout – arrangement of text and graphics

Liquid Crystal Display (LCD) – screen type used in laptops and for flat panel monitors

Liteware – a free version of a program which is missing some high-end or desirable features

Logon – procedure where the user must identify himself to the computer to continue

Macro – small program to automate actions within a major application

Main Memory – where the computer stores the data and commands that are currently being used, also know as RAM (random access memory)

Margin – space at the borders of the page or other document object

Megabyte (MB) – 1024 kilobytes historically. For data storage devices and telecommunications, a megabyte is one million (1,000,000) bytes

Megahertz (Mhz) – 1 million cycles per second

Memory Management – program to handle where RAM programs put their data

Menu – a list of available commands which may contain other commands as a submenu

Modem – the device which translates between the analog phone line and the digital computer. From Modulate/ Demodulate

Motherboard – main circuit board of the computer

Nag Screen – screen message that reminds you to pay up each time you run a shareware program

Nanosecond (Ns) – 1 billionth of a second. Used to measure memory speed

Nesting – putting directories or folders inside other directories or folders

Network – a set of computers that are linked together on a permanent basis

Newsgroup – a discussion group on the Internet where messages and responses are posted for all to read

Node – each device connected to a network

OCR Software – software which changes a scanned document from an image to editable text

Operating System – the instructions that the computer uses to tell itself how it works

Orientation – direction the printed page runs: portrait or landscape

Output – data that has been processed into useful form

Partition – a portion of a hard disk. Disks have separate partitions for different operating systems or to store data separately

Paste – place clipboard contents at cursor location

Pixel – one dot on a screen, comes from picture element

PPM – pages per minute. Measures printer speed

Print Preview – displays how the document will print as opposed to how it looks on the screen

Query – a way to arrange records in a particular kind of order, or to only show the records that match certain criteria

Queue – the set of print jobs waiting to be done

RAM – main memory (random access memory), which is volatile memory that is erased when power is turned off

ROM – read only memory that cannot be changed. Contains the instructions to start the computer

Refresh Rate – how often the picture is redrawn on a monitor

Removable Media – storage media that are removed from the computer, such as flash drives, CDs and DVDs

Router – connects networks and controls the traffic of data among the networks

Scanner – a device that captures a whole page and converts it to digital image

Server – a computer which handles network tasks and data

Shareware – software which you may try for a limited time before purchasing

Shut Down – close all programs and turn off computer

Soft Copy – displayed on screen or by other non-permanent means

Spacing – space between letters or lines of text

Spell Checker – the program which looks for spelling errors

Spreadsheet – program for handling numeric data, like budgets, financial statements and sales records

SQL – structured query language for commands that create database queries

Table – a set of rows and columns

Touchscreen – monitor screen that reacts to being touched by a finger

Tower – Vertical case for a personal computer

Trojan – short for Trojan horse, a program that allows others to access your data, to record your logins and passwords, or to destroy or alter data

Typeface – a set of characters of similar design

Undo – reverses whatever change you just made

Upgrade – to replace a program with a newer version of one you already have

Upload – transfer a file from your computer to another

USB – Universal Serial Bus, a connection that can be used by a wide range of devices, rather than each device having a unique connector

User Profile – a set of preferences for a particular user.

Utility – a program that performs tasks related to maintaining your computer's health - hardware or data

Vector – a means of defining an image in terms of geometric shapes. Used by drawing programs

Virus – a computer program that performs tasks without your consent. May be harmless but annoying or may be highly damaging.

Window – a rectangular area of the screen that displays a program's user interface, a document, or a system message

Wizard – an automatic set of steps that lead you through a process

Word Wrap – automatically wrapping the text to the next line so it all fits within the page

Worm – An unwanted program that duplicates itself across a network. It uses up storage space and resources and can interfere with the ability of the system to function

Write Protect – a method that keeps data from being over-written

WYSIWYG – what you see is what you get, displaying results on the monitor as they will appear when printed

Index